The Blood Is
Wild

also by
Don and Bridget MacCaskill

WILD ENDEAVOUR
ON THE SWIRL OF THE TIDE

The Blood Is Wild

Bridget MacCaskill

With photographs by Don MacCaskill

JONATHAN CAPE
LONDON

First published 1995

1 3 5 7 9 10 8 6 4 2

© Bridget MacCaskill 1995
Photographs © Don MacCaskill 1995

Bridget MacCaskill has asserted her right
under the Copyright, Designs and Patents Act, 1988
to be identified as the author of this work

First published in the United Kingdom in 1995 by
Jonathan Cape
Random House, 20 Vauxhall Bridge Road, London SW1V 2SA

Random House Australia (Pty) Limited
20 Alfred Street, Milsons Point, Sydney,
New South Wales 2061, Australia

Random House New Zealand Limited
18 Poland Road, Glenfield,
Auckland 10, New Zealand

Random House South Africa (Pty) Limited
PO Box 337, Bergvlei, South Africa

Random House UK Limited Reg. No. 954009

A CIP catalogue record for this book
is available from the British Library

ISBN 0–224–03698–X (cased)
ISBN 0–224–03697–1 (paperback)

Typeset by SX Composing Ltd, Rayleigh, Essex
Printed in Great Britain by
Mackays of Chatham PLC,
Chatham, Kent

Contents

Illustrations

The female buzzard
Male buzzard bringing food to the nest
Eagle pair on the eyrie with chicks
Eaglet at six weeks old
The injured eaglet which recovered
Fully feathered eaglet, ready to fly

Introduction

THE RED FOX (*Vulpes vulpes*) inspires either love and respect for its beauty, intelligence and resilience, or a kind of obsessive hatred in those who regard it as a threat to their livelihood in some form or other. It is a carnivore (though berries and fruit are much enjoyed when available), and is well-equipped for efficient hunting, with long legs capable of quick bursts of speed, a long pointed muzzle which is extremely sensitive to scent, and ears which are capable of picking up the slightest sound. The fox hunts, like all other predatory species, in order to survive and it predates upon, or scavenges, whatever is there. It was inevitable, therefore, that when man began to farm livestock there would be conflict. As the scale of farming grew with the demands of expanding human populations, so the problem escalated, particularly when the fox was deprived by man of its natural prey, such as the rabbit through myxomatosis.

The fox and the fox controversy have always interested us and inspired our many years of study of this much-maligned mammal. We live in the Highlands of Scotland, a predominantly sheep-rearing and sport-orientated region where persecution has made the fox even more shy and elusive than elsewhere. What we discovered over a long period has been put together in this book to make one continuous whole. Much was learned from the waifs that came our way. Some of them were kept in as 'wild' conditions as possible with the minimum of human contact. Others, unashamedly, became pets. The story revolves around Rufus and Rusty, two delightful fox cubs who shared our lives for a while, and some of the creatures that shared the hills and glens with them.

'Until he extends his circle of compassion to
all living things, man will not himself find peace.'
Dr Albert Schweitzer

ONE

Wild Waifs

GREAT BANKS OF CUMULUS, shafted in pink and red, billowed over distant mountains and ridges and a pulsating, golden sun was sinking into the fiery furnace behind. Rock-ravaged gullies, which split the hillsides asunder, were already deep in shadow, and sombre cliffs, woods of oak and birch were all fast fading into the mists of evening. A dark ribbon, mysteriously meandering along the bottom of the glen, was a large burn on its way to a nearby loch. Utter stillness was broken only by the soft twitterings of a sleepy wren and a croak from a raven flying home to roost. It was a sublime moment on a Highland hillside with kindly shades of night creeping in to embrace all who would slumber there, and conceal those who must hunt to survive.

We had come slowly and stealthily, stalking into the wind as silently as human beings can, our objective a fox's den near the top of the glen. In January we had heard the bloodcurdling shrieks of the vixen as she called to her mate and his excited yelps as he replied. Each evening their wild courting song had echoed eerily over the hillsides, now from the lower wooded slopes, now from the rocky ridges above. Sometimes we heard them at dawn as well. The wild wooing of winter should have led to a mating and by now, in the second half of May, the cubs should be about five or six weeks old. If the pair were using this den, then we could hope to see the young out and crawling around at its entrance. That is, if the fox hunters had left them alone.

In the Highlands, hatred of the fox is almost a part of countryside culture. Preventing predation upon lambs in the spring is the most common excuse for almost relentless persecution, though preservation of grouse and other game birds, and even domestic hens and ducks, come a close second. Destruction of dens, snaring, gassing, poisoning, hunting on foot with hounds, are all methods considered acceptable by most estate owners. Traditional dens are inspected each spring after the cubs are born, usually by shepherds or gamekeepers, and the occupants of those in use destroyed.

These uncomfortable facts were much in mind as we crept into our hiding place in a jumble of rocks on the hillside. We stood for a moment, admiring the dramatic dying of the day, then turned to see how it all looked at the den. The backdrop was reassuringly the same as ever – monstrous rocks, silhouetted now against an angry sky, brooding over the entrance below. It was when binoculars were lowered to the gaping hole beneath that delight on this beautiful evening turned to disgust. It was as if a small whirlwind had been at work. Soil at the entrance, which should have been padded down hard with the comings and goings of a family of foxes, was broken up and scattered by the kicking and scraping of frantic feet. Terriers! In front, where the ground sloped away to the forest below, the vegetation was trampled and torn as if a bloody battle had been fought. A vixen bolted, and at bay? And there lay the evidence, unmistakable and irrevocable – three small fox cubs carelessly draped over the knife-edge top of a rock close by. The fox hunters had been at work.

'Not again!' I exclaimed, sickened by a sight I never became used to.

Don made no reply. He began walking quickly towards the den. I followed more slowly, reluctant to know the worst, especially when he deviated to examine something a few yards down the hillside. The vixen was dead, all right. She lay in a coffin of straggling heather, shot through the head, her beautiful brush cut off for the bounty. Unconscious of indignity, she rested belly up, nipples still sore though she would have been well on with weaning the cubs, head at an awkward angle, eyes staring, and her mouth open in a ghastly grimace. We searched for the body of her mate, knowing that a marksman would have stayed behind to catch him as he brought food for his family, but we found nothing. Perhaps, this time, he had been lucky.

'Dear God!' I exploded, when a few minutes later we were

bending to examine the poor mutilated bodies of the cubs. 'Will they never learn?'

'Not in our time I reckon,' Don said sadly.

Many and terrible are the tales told of the sins of the fox, especially in connection with their predation upon lambs. Much research has been done into the habits and diet of the animal which proves that, though it does sometimes take a live lamb, it is comparatively seldom. More often the dead ones are taken as carrion. The evidence, scientific and objective, is readily available but rarely read or believed by those with a vested interest in killing foxes. They just do not want to know.

'It seems so unnecessary,' I added bitterly as Don bent low to the mouth of the den.

'Hush,' he whispered impatiently. 'I can hear a cub.'

Sure enough, a faint squeaking came from somewhere in the depths of the hole. It was almost inaudible but plaintive, and definitely there. The vixen would have been panicked into flight by terriers put in for the purpose; she would have been shot when, at last, she bolted; the terriers would have been sent down again to finish off the cubs. A bloody business. This time, however, one had somehow survived.

'Can we get hold of it?' I asked anxiously.

'We'll have a go, anyway,' said Don. 'I'll try and reach it, but see if you can find some wire, just in case.'

The hunt for wire on a bare and rocky hillside was not as ridiculous as it might seem. The forest fence was only a few hundred yards down the hill and discarded pieces were quite likely to be lying around. I found a coil of it after only a few minutes' search and with Don's wire-cutters, always carried in case we could free some wretched creature caught in a snare, quickly cut off a six-foot length. As I walked back to the den I straightened it and scratched one end with a knife to be as rough and serrated as possible.

Don had had no success, and there was no sound now from within the hole. I imagined the cub, terrified, hungry, and waiting in vain for a mother who would not return, lying in a cleft where the dogs had been unable to get at it – nor humans either. It had probably been there no more than a couple of days and might still have a chance if only we could somehow get it out. I handed over the wire and knew it would be a ticklish business, for a fox den could have several inaccessible chambers within and the little one, retreating from exploring human fingers or a probing wire, might well reverse out of reach. In a few minutes, however, there was a sudden exclamation.

'I've found it,' Don said quietly.

'Do be careful,' I implored, quite unnecessarily since he had done this job often before, but thinking of a helpless mite being poked about by something alarming and strange.

Now he was gently twisting the wire this way and that, feeling cautiously for a hold. I wondered how the fur of a soft and woolly baby coat could possibly be caught by this seemingly unlikely means.

'I've got it,' whispered Don.

Slowly, with infinite care, he drew the creature towards him and in a few seconds a small bundle could just be seen in the dark depths of the hole. As it was pulled closer and closer, I got ready to put in my hand to collect it. Then, all of a sudden, there was a hitch. The animal was stuck! There seemed no good reason for it. It had lain quite still, apparently long past caring what happened to it. There had been no struggling. Now it could be persuaded no farther.

Don swore. 'Bloody hell!'

'What's happened?'

'I think there's a piece of rock sticking out into the passage and the cub won't slip over it. I'm afraid of losing contact. Do you think you could reach it?'

While Don held the wire still, I poked in a cautious arm, running my fingers over dried-up soil and stones to find the way, until at last, when I was just about running out of stretch, they made contact. The small body was warm and breathing.

'I've got it,' I whispered. 'It's still alive!'

Afraid of not getting a proper hold, so that the animal might drop out of reach, I felt about for a leg or some other part which could be gripped easily. I found a paw, tried a gentle pull, and got nipped for my pains. Alive, all right. Gradually, little by little, the soft handful was gathered in.

'What a darling,' I crooned idiotically when at last it was out and I was wrapping it into the folds of the sweater I had taken off.

'Quick!' Don exclaimed impatiently. 'There's another.'

This one was no problem. Both cubs, weak with hunger, must have been crawling towards the entrance to try and find their mother, and the second, creeping after its sibling, was easily secured. Don placed it beside the other. There was no more squeaking from within the den, and in any case, it was most unlikely that the vixen's family had exceeded five. That was the lot.

'Right,' he said. 'Let's have a look at them.'

Both cubs lay motionless, eyes tight closed and only faintly breathing, as if the experience of the last few minutes had been too much.

'It's a while since those two were fed,' I observed.

'Better get them home as fast as possible.'

We wasted no more time. Each little scrap was tucked into the warmth beneath our sweaters and, with tightened belts to prevent them slipping, and a hand to protect them from too much bouncing about, we set off as fast as possible down the glen. As we climbed the stile at the forest fence, I glanced back towards the crag beneath which lay their home. Its great rocks, in the fading light, mocked me. What are you so upset about, they seemed to say. Four creatures are dead. Two are alive. Human beings have been at work. We have seen it all before. It has always been so. I could almost imagine gigantic shoulders in a mighty shrug of indifference.

I hurried down the forest ride after Don. The tall, dark stems drew closer together in the gathering gloom, so it seemed, and feelings of dismay were compounded by the claustrophobic canopy overhead. Once across the wet meadows below – a stumbling, slithering, cursing business, hanging on to tiny waifs and searching for secure footing as well – the walking was easier and the mood lifted. We hurried along the well-known track, the cheerful chuckling of the burn our guide and the star-chequered beginnings of night good omens that our orphans would survive. Monster boulders, distinctive in size and shape, and old friends, marked our progress down the way, and in the shelter of an outcrop I checked the breathing of a bundle held against my ribs.

At last we reached our van which was parked beside the forest gate. Once in it I held both cubs nestled in a rug on my lap and defended them, as best I could, from the bumpy ride home.

Forty minutes later we arrived home at our old, sturdily-built stone farmhouse, surrounded by woods of larch and pine. A welcoming plume from the Aga chimney drifted into the air.

Once in the large, comfortable old kitchen, we slid into the familiar routine rehearsed each time we attempted the rescue of a wild creature. Out came the old box which had been specially made for the purpose. It was deep-sided and about five feet long by three wide, with a lid of steel mesh for ventilation which could be covered by a blanket when necessary. Plenty of newspaper in the bottom, crumpled on top of two hot water bottles placed a little apart, made it a reasonable replacement for a den. Our two charges weighed in at 2lb 8oz, a male, and 2lb 4oz, a female, and were compared with the weekly records we had kept of cubs previously reared. It seemed that they must indeed be between five and six weeks old.

We had two dogs at the time, a golden labrador bitch called Shuna, who was the gentlest of creatures in spite of her size, and a young collie, Shian, who, though never a working dog, had retained much of that breed's instincts to round up and watch over any creatures, including humans, that were a part of her daily life. Both were used to taking on the duties of foster parent, and though neither would be able to feed our waifs, they were adept at keeping them warm and clean. We called to Shuna and, with a look we could only call resigned, she hopped in beside the cubs and settled around them. When she began gently to pant, we removed the hot bottles.

Food was the next priority. At five weeks their mother would have almost finished weaning them and be bringing in the voles, hares, rabbits and so on that she had either caught herself or her mate had brought to her. By now, the cubs' sharp little teeth would be well able to tear and chew. For the moment, though, until they regained some strength, they must have something easily digested and sustaining. We made up a mixture from lamb feed, which would be as rich as the mother's milk, poured it into two squash bottles and attached the teats which we always had handy for these occasions.

The half-starved infants had no inhibitions. The delicious smell, not too unlike that of their mother's milk, was all that was required. Each teat was greedily snatched, two pairs of paws began urgently to knead, and soft sucking sounds soon filled the air. We allowed each 4oz, thinking of stomachs not filled for some time, and planned to increase the quantity with each feed. Meantime, satisfied and sleepy, they sank down into their newspaper bed and Shian hopped in beside them to take her turn as nursemaid. She licked them clean, the small bodies unresisting and already asleep, then she too closed her eyes.

At last we could relax and take a proper look at our fox cubs. The male, unlike his sister, had a thick white tip to his brush. Long guard hairs were beginning to grow in on their coats and the rufous fur that would replace the dark grey wool of babyhood was already showing. The dog fox was a comic sight with a patch of tawny fur over one eye, one ear erect, even in sleep, the other flopping forward. Both muzzles were lengthening into the true, sharp 'foxy' face of the adult, and their eyes, which had opened only briefly when feeding, were changing from blue to smoky brown. We gently prized their jaws apart and examined the teeth which had nipped us earlier. They were well-developed and would certainly have been coping with meat by now. We named the cubs, Rufus and Rusty.

Shian was relieved of her duties at bedtime. We refilled the two hot water bottles, covered them with more newspaper and an old blanket, then placed our charges in the nice warm nest. We took it in turns to feed them during the night and already they were beginning to be more lively. The male was precocious compared with his sister, tottering about the box, nipping her to try and persuade her to play with him, and finding the newsprint great fun to tear and chew. She was weaker than he and just sat on her hunkers yawning mightily before collapsing once again into sleep. Both Don and I were accepted as surrogate mothers and were greeted with open mouths and wildly wagging tails whenever we arrived with the squash bottles.

Our orphans made steady progress during the following day. Milk was still greedily accepted but small offerings of mince were instantly seized and demolished in a twinkling. The dogs took turns as nannies, cleaning them up after feeds and curling around them afterwards to sleep. It was interesting that neither of the fox cubs had any fear of their foster parents – perhaps each had a nice motherly smell about her. By evening the cubs were very much as they should be at their age, full of beans and playing rolling-over, kicking and nipping games, much as small pups or kittens would do, still creeping about the box to sniff and explore, and churning their mysteriously noisy newspaper bed into a fine mess.

We watched them as we ate our evening meal and the thought occurred to me that a little more exercise might be a good idea.

'Shall we see if they had already been coming out of their den?' I joked, thinking of their likely behaviour in the wild.

'It's your kitchen,' retorted Don, knowing well what fox cubs might do in only a short time.

'They're still very small,' I said, laughing. 'We'll risk it.'

We lifted out the babes and while Don held them I quickly turned the box on its side so that the lid became a ramp down which they could crawl. The newspaper nest now rested on one of the sides. Don popped the family back and we waited to see what would happen.

Response was immediate. Rufus, already a bold fellow, pricked up his ears and sat gazing with great interest at the fascinating world that was our kitchen. With no hesitation at all he set off to prospect, placing all four paws on the top of the ramp and eagerly taking two steps forward. Disaster. At once, with legs helplessly splayed, he skidded all the way down to the bottom where he lay kicking and trying in vain to roll over on to his feet. Righted at last, he took a cautious, creepy-crawling sort of a step across the floor. Disaster again. This was a strange and slippery place, not at all like the roughened soil at the entrance to his den. Once more he lay struggling on his back.

The young cub was puzzled but not hurt. Very soon he was up again and sitting nonchalantly scratching one of his ears with a hind foot. Then, curiosity overcoming caution, he started to reconnoitre again. He did better this time. The first few steps were felt for carefully and tested out. Then, as his legs gained strength, so his confidence grew. Very soon he was toddling all over the room.

'He'd been coming out of the den, all right,' I laughed, as we turned to see how Rusty was getting on.

'She'll follow his example,' said Don, smiling. 'We're going to regret this, you know.'

Rusty had watched her sibling's ridiculous antics but, more timid than he, had remained firmly in the box. It took her another ten minutes to make up her mind. Then, much more tentatively, she made the hazardous journey to the floor. Soon, still on unsteady legs, both were crawling, wobbly-walking, shuffling all over the kitchen. Inquisitive noses poked into everything that caught their fancy and even the lino was scraped at diligently, as if they could not understand why it did not behave just like the soil at their den. Shuna, lying full length in front of the fire, was trampled all over and nipped unmercifully. She never turned a hair, and only an angelic nature would have put up with this treatment. Rufus found an old tennis ball and recoiled in alarm when it went running away. Immediately curious, he went scampering after it, patting it, falling on his side to kick it, and soon was playing a foxy version of a game of football. Rusty, plain startled, ran back to her den.

Half an hour had gone by when I accidentally dropped a teaspoon. As it clattered to the floor Rufus, immediately scared, scurried to join his sister and buried his small head beneath the newspaper. Already the box was a 'safe place' in which to shelter. In minutes both had collapsed and were fast asleep.

We set off on a routine mopping up.

'Right!' I said, when at last half a dozen small puddles and two messes, all smelling strongly of fox, had been cleared away. 'It's out in the shed for them!'

Don chuckled. 'Shall we put them out tonight?'

'Tomorrow will do. Let's shut them in the box for now.'

A final glance at two innocents, eyes tight closed and breathing regularly, a word to the dogs to go to their beds, on guard, and we hurried off to bed.

The shed acted as a kind of clearing house for any wild creatures we were hoping to nurse back to health. At the end of their time in it, they would either be released as close as possible to the spot where they had originally been discovered, or put into a much larger run to live out their lives in as congenial surroundings as we could devise. The first alternative depended very much on the animal involved and the degree of injury it had sustained – deer, for instance, have no enemies, except in the shooting season, so are not a problem. If a release were possible, human contact with the animal (though to some extent inevitable), would be limited to the minimum. In that way, it was hoped, no bond would develop and no trust in the human species be established.

The fox belongs to the second category. In the wild, these animals have total distrust of human beings and go to any lengths to avoid them. You would think them prime candidates for release. Unfortunately, those that have been kept in captivity for any length of time learn in some degree to trust human beings. It is almost impossible to avoid this. Young cubs become so tame they are just like domestic dogs and it is difficult to resist the temptation to bring them into the home to join other pets, to take them for walks with the dogs, and even to travel with them on a jaunt in a motor vehicle. This last they love. Foxes have delightful, affectionate, even trusting natures and, of course, in the end do not know the difference between human beings and themselves. If liberated, they are a very bad bet in the survival stakes. Sooner or later they will fall foul of man and be shot, or worse. With Rufus and Rusty, there was really no decision to make. So young now, they would become totally imprinted on us and extremely tame. We would give them the best life we could in as natural surroundings as possible – within an enclosure.

For the moment, though, it would be a short stay in the hut where we could be sure that both were feeding properly and that there were no injuries so far not discovered. The next morning, when Don returned from an early walk, I asked him if it was ready, remembering various household articles stored there.

'Sure,' he replied. 'Everything is up on the rafters.'

After breakfast, we carried our wards to their new home in the garden. There was an open box in one corner of the hut, raised a little against draughts, with a sloping ramp leading to the floor. It was almost full of straw into which they could burrow for warmth or to hide when alarmed. The floor was covered with an old piece of linoleum, for easy cleaning, and the door had a 'cat flap' which could be hinged open. This led into a small run, wired against climbing and tunnelling, which would do for exercise until they were well-established and big enough to be put into their permanent home in the large run. The cubs took to their new abode at once, walking about all over it and sniffing enquiringly at whatever scents lingered there from other temporary inhabitants. Stronger now, after food and rest, they trotted out into the run and up on to a large log we had put there for games. We threw them a haunch of rabbit and immediately they were fighting over it, trying to grab and pull away, chittering angrily, growling, snapping, barging. No doubt at all, they knew all about rabbit and how to scrap for it.

'Hurry and get another piece, for heaven's sake,' I yelled at Don, who was outside the run. 'Rusty won't get any at this rate.'

Soon two fierce little cubs were hungrily devouring their breakfasts, Rusty doing as well as her greedy brother. Once he tried to steal a morsel, creeping towards it and pretending he had no interest in it, but she responded with fierce growls, yanking her piece away and turning her rump to him. I put down two separate bowls of milk in opposite corners and hoped she would be smart enough to get her share. Then we left them alone to explore their new surroundings and to work off high spirits.

The cubs grew fast and in two weeks were tearing out to greet whoever brought their food, white-tipped tail and dark one wagging energetically, and each with an absurd grin on its face. They seemed to enjoy being handled or played with, and very soon it was as well to wear a pair of stout gloves against their sharp teeth. They still slept a lot, quite often with one of the dogs, ate voraciously, and seemed happy enough playing strenuous games of I-am-king-of-the-castle all over the logs, chasing each other round and round the run, and practising boxing and biting techniques. For a while, at least, they were content and should not get into too much mischief.

We ought to have known better, of course. One morning, a week or two later, I went out as usual to give the cubs their first meal of the day, to lift the cat flap and to clean up. As I opened the door, two ruffians came rushing to greet me, running over my feet in their haste to get out into the run. The scene, inside, had me slamming it again hastily. I threw them their rabbit pieces and rushed back to the house.

'It's today for the big run,' I shouted to Don, who was still upstairs, shaving.

'What's happened?'

'Come and see.'

After finishing a painting job, the evening before, he had absent-mindedly placed a ladder against one of the walls inside the hut, quite forgetting what even very young foxes could get up to. It was an old-fashioned wooden affair, that ladder, with steps roughened and worn over many years. You've guessed it! The cubs must have been quick to discover a new and exciting game. After tentative hops on and off the bottom step, they grew bold. Foxes are good climbers and in no time at all the youngsters were scrambling higher and higher on steps that gave secure hold to sharp claws. Once safely at the top, it was an easy leap on to a rafter. There, for our sins, an old mattress and two ancient pillows straddled the beams. Teeth and claws had gone to work. Maybe a single feather floating gently to the floor had been watched with curiosity. Then another and another, soft and unpredictable in flight. Patting paws went to work. Finally, with claws tearing at mattress and pillows, a wonderful, mysterious cloud of floating fluffy feathers had drifted slowly down to join the others gone before.

We could not help laughing. Feathers were clinging to the rough boarding of the walls, lining the window sill, carpeting the floor, and still bulging from the gaping holes out of which they had been torn. They were even in the cubs' sleeping box and their flattened appearance suggested that Rufus and Rusty, at last exhausted, had discovered how comfortable a feather bed could be. Now, as we pottered about looking at the damage, small whirlwinds of feathers and dust stirred into the air, to float prettily on shafts of sunlight to the floor.

'Right, you two,' said Don, as the cubs came running up to him, having demolished their pieces of rabbit. 'It's more than time for the big run.'

Uttering the friendly keening sounds that foxes make when 'talking' to friends, both rolled over on to their backs to have their tummies tickled. Frenzied screams of delight welcomed this attention which they always demanded whenever we arrived. We carried them back into the hut to see what they would do. Both instantly remembered their wonderful frolic and set off again, rampaging round and round, chasing feathers and trying to catch them, jumping in and out of their feather bed, even climbing the ladder again. At last, when Don and I were both sneezing and spluttering with the dust, this energetic pair grew tired. As the feathers began to settle once more we picked up two panting, unresisting morsels, pinned each under an arm, and carried them over to their new home.

The big run had been constructed some years before to accommodate our various waifs and was as good an imitation of a wild place as we could devise. Deer fencing had been used to enclose about an acre of wooded hillside, just beyond our garden, and a substantial overhang had been added to prevent any but the most agile of animals climbing over and out. A length of netting was continued down into the ground and inwards for a considerable distance, so that a serious attempt to tunnel out ought to be spotted in time and the earthworks blocked. As part of a natural outcrop of rock beneath a couple of tall Scots pines, we had built an artificial den from boulders, turf and any other suitable material to hand. Its various inhabitants over the years had probably improved the interior and no doubt there were tunnels and chambers below. One or two birches had been cut on the perimeter of the run to discourage acrobatic escapes, but the rest contained a scattering of these trees, with rowan, ash and some oak as well. Bracken, scrub willow, nettles and various grasses provided good cover, especially in summer.

We opened the gate and placed the cubs inside. Rufus, always the bolder of the two, put his nose to the ground and straight away ran off to investigate. He paused once to look back, as if seeking reassurance, then vanished out of sight into the bracken. Rusty, more timid, sat a minute making up her mind. Then she, too, set off, with nose sniffing eagerly, to follow her brother into a new and fascinating world. I imagined them poking inquisitive noses into inviting new scents, parting the vegetation to look cautiously beyond, scraping the soil to get at some interesting scent beneath – perhaps their first experience of the voles they would later hunt as a matter of course. We waited a few more minutes to make sure all was well, then left them to it.

'They'll be fine,' said Don confidently. 'Not much mischief they can get up to now.'

'I've heard that before,' I said.

That evening I put out two portions of rabbit, as usual, and when Don went over later to see if all was well, he found that they had been removed elsewhere. When he called to the cubs, they came dashing to greet him with squeals of delight, but stayed only briefly, suddenly running off again into the bracken where a narrow fox track had been worn already. They did not reappear. Fox affairs were now evidently much more important than human beings. We took it as a sign that they had well and truly settled down.

Rufus and Rusty would not gain much experience of stalking and killing larger prey. There would be voles to catch, until they became scarce, and they would learn to dig for earthworms and beetles, but otherwise their food would be brought to them each evening. In the wild, the vixen and dog would still have been bringing prey, dropping it somewhere close to the den, and to a chirruping call the cubs would come running to squabble for a share. Their mother, by her own example, would have been encouraging them to hunt small items in the near vicinity of the den, and in late summer they would discover that berries, especially the blaeberry, were good to eat. Gradually, as they grew bigger and more adventurous, prompted by hunger and parents who no longer brought them food, they would venture farther and farther afield to learn of bigger prey to be hunted and carrion to be discovered.

From now on Rufus and Rusty lived a life that was a compromise between the natural one they would have led in the wild, and that enforced on them by captivity. As they grew older, it was late dusk before they became active, and we often heard the sounds of noisy games as we lay in bed. The vegetation became threaded with little paths, soon bare and padded down, and experimental holes began to appear all over the place. Every evening we watched them tearing round and round the run, in and out of the den, and even, when one was desperate to escape the other, up one of the birch trees. The rocky mound of the den was romped all over, stones and rubble sliding to the bottom and having to be repaired most days. If called, they would usually come running, either for food or for a brief greeting, but as we departed we always saw them returning to the den or curling to sleep in a favourite hollow close by. Night was the proper time for foxes!

Digging holes became a frequent pastime. Sometimes it was just a shallow affair into which a bone or a piece of fur was scraped, then roughly covered over, the instinct to cache surplus food already there. Sometimes it was as if they were digging for earthworms – something also that would come to them naturally. A leap and a pounce was probably after a vole, still rashly existing within the run, though we never actually saw one being eaten. Some excavations were quite deep with an impressive scattering of stones and rubble all around. These were usually close to the fence. Master tunnellers at work! We quickly filled in such holes, discouraging a second attempt with a heavy boulder. The little male was developing into a fine young fellow, face now sharp and pointed, ears erect, white-tipped tail thick and bushy, dark feet and forelegs strong as steel. The female had similar markings, except for her tail, but it looked as though she would always be small, even for a vixen.

One night we were woken by the customary yelps and screams which accompanied those strenuous games in the fox run, but, barely awake, it seemed to me the sound was more hysterical than usual.

'Listen to that!' I nudged Don into wakefulness.

'What?' he asked sleepily.

'Rufus and Rusty. Can't you hear them?'

'Sounds as though one of them is being murdered,' he muttered as he turned over.

I lay awake listening, more and more convinced that this was not the regular evening performance. At last, I could stay in bed no longer. Summer days in the Highlands are long and, though it was now shortly before midnight, there was still enough light by which to see.

'Let's go down to the run,' I suggested as the clamour continued.

'Why?' Don enquired without enthusiasm.

'Maybe there's someone there.'

'Surely not.' Then, seeds of doubt sprouting, he mumbled, 'I suppose we'd better make sure.'

We slipped on jeans and sweaters over our night gear. Once in the garden we instinctively paused to test the wind – a light breeze blowing from the run towards us. If a strange animal was causing the commotion then we would have a good chance of discovering it before it discovered us. The outrageous sounds continued – two little fox cubs screaming their heads off about something that was driving them frantic. We crawled into some bushes at the end of the garden, and from there could see quite a large part of the run.

It was, indeed, a gripping drama. Rufus and Rusty were positively screeching with excitement, running at the gate, leaping up and down it, and even trying to tunnel under it. A large fox, almost certainly a male, was head down to it and nosing inquisitively through the netting. He seemed both curious and friendly, perhaps because these were cubs, sniffing and snuffling busily to get their scent, a grin on his face as if he were greeting friends, though his ears were laid back and his tail was swishing busily from side to side. Then away they all went, charging along the fence, the cubs shrieking with excitement, the dog also, but less high-pitched: let's meet, let's meet. Up and down they tore, becoming more and more frenzied, until we wondered when a serious attempt might be made to climb over the top. All of a sudden, perhaps growing bored or frustrated, the big dog turned away. He lifted a leg to mark a nearby tree stump then, without a backward glance, trotted off into the forest. The cubs stood panting, watching him go, and then, the fun over, they ran back along a path which led to their den.

'What a carry-on,' I said as we walked back through the old garden. 'Could that possibly have been their father?'

'Perhaps,' replied Don. 'It certainly looked like him. To a dog fox, the distance would be nothing. This is probably part of his range, anyway.'

'Would he recognise his own cubs?'

'I shouldn't think so. He'd have had little contact with them by the time the den was destroyed.'

'It's a nice thought, anyway,' I said happily.

TWO

Glimpses of Gold

WHILE RUFUS AND RUSTY were settling down at home, we were also busy with the usual ploys of spring and early summer. All the fox dens in the area had to be looked at in case a vixen had, against the odds, managed to rear a family. We also checked the eagle eyries for signs of use and kept an eye open for buzzard, hen harrier, kestrel and any other raptors which might be present. This year there was a bonus. A fox den in a wild and rocky corrie near the top of Gleann na h-Iolaire, the Glen of the Eagle, looked promising, and one of the eyries there had been built up and was probably in use. Both, if young were successfully raised, might give us some fascinating watching and maybe some interesting interaction between the two species. Late on a beautiful afternoon in mid-June we set off to see what we could see.

It was a great day for a long tramp, cooler than of late, with a breeze blowing in our faces from the north. We planned to spend the night out so that we could watch the den late into the evening and, if the eagles had nested and were rearing a family, we would watch the eyrie from our hide the next morning at dawn. We locked the van, yanked backpacks into place, then stood for a minute admiring the five old pines which guarded the entrance to the glen. They grew on a rocky knoll where lambs were playing tig in and out of the tall, straight stems, their mothers, hardy black-faced ewes, placidly dozing in the shade beneath. Ridges, rugged on each side, tumbled to the valley bottom in jumbles of great granite boulders, and graceful birch and rowan dotted the hillsides. A mountain burn, clear and sparkling in the sunshine, splashed prettily over sculpted rock to join the large, placid loch behind us. To its chuckling music we set off along the narrow track which bordered one of its banks.

A family of dippers came too. First a youngster, still in juvenile feathering, skimming the dancing waters, then alighting on a rock perch right in the centre of the burn. It curtseyed up and down, up and down to the shimmering waters, as if life depended on it. Then a second one came flitting as low and shadowing its sibling, to settle on another boulder close to the bank. Both were anxiously looking downstream. Suddenly they began to cheep excitedly, bobbing up and down so hard that they must surely fall in. Two adults, darkly chestnut and with startling white breasts, came swiftly flying towards them, each with a beakful of juicy morsels. They briefly dowsed the insects in the water, passed them over into widely gaping mouths, then without further ado slanted away again, presumably to catch the next meal.

'Hard work keeping those two satisfied,' I commented, laughing at the greedy way the food was gobbled.

'They'll soon be managing for themselves,' said Don. 'Come on. We haven't time to waste.'

As we moved on up the burn, so the young dippers glided with us, as yet too small to venture into its frothing waters, but streaking between one rock stance and the next. Always they kept just ahead, enticing us towards the tantalising distant hills. We came to an old stone bridge and knelt beside the ancient arch to look underneath. There on a shelf in a dark corner fringed with fern, and cunningly built in a cavity between two large stones, was a beautifully constructed nest. It was dome-shaped, mostly of moss, and was undoubtedly the birthplace of our little dippers. Very shortly, as we continued on our way, they performed a cheeky U-turn with fast-fluttering wings and flew back the way they had come. Perhaps their parents had called.

As we walked on into the breeze the glen began gradually to narrow, the path become rougher and the burn more turbulent. We noted a small group of deer high on the west ridge and sheep grazing on the hillsides to the east. Meadow pipits, wheatears and larks darted here, there, and everywhere catching insects for hungry families. There was a fleeting glimpse of a small bright green dragon as a lizard skidded suddenly away from a rock to the right of the path and, in spite of our best endeavours, could not be found again. From a small wood of oak in the lower reaches of a gully came an angry squawk as we passed, a hoodie crow warning its fledglings of our coming. Objecting all the while, 'greyback' rose into the air with fast-flapping wings, flew higher up the gully to settle on the topmost branches of another ancient tree, and shouted the odds until our presence ceased to bother it.

The hillside to our left was broken by rocky outcrops and scatterings of rowan and birch. From a marshy place below them a heron flew out of a patch of reeds protesting indignantly. Uncanny eyesight had probably seen us long ago but we had not spotted it. Now we were too close for comfort and it flew with deliberate wingbeats towards the top of the glen.

'I wonder if there's a pair nesting up one of those gullies,' said Don.

'Surely that's unlikely,' I protested. 'There aren't any suitable trees and there can't be much of a food supply so far from the loch.'

'Not so far for a bird with big wings,' teased Don.

'The young will have flown by now, anyway,' I persisted.

'Maybe. We'll check those gullies next year, just in case.'

We watched the source of our difference of opinion alight, with furiously-flapping wings and long legs dancing to find secure footing, in another boggy area farther up the glen. When later we passed the spot the big grey bird, head down, formidable bill ready to strike, was concentrating hard upon something at its feet, perhaps a frog. This time we were no longer important and it did not stir.

All the while we were gaining height, the glen sweeping northwest and then north and becoming more bare and rocky. Eventually we stopped for a breather just below the brooding cliffs where the eagles had their eyrie. Giant outcrops, with boulders tumbling down the slopes to the burn below, decorated the hillside and were impressive guardians of an eagle fortress. Here, after a spell, we would break away from the path to begin the scramble up the hillside. Backpacks were thrown off, and while Don set up his telescope on its tripod, I trained binoculars on to the corrie where the fox den was situated.

'The eyrie looks promising,' Don remarked after a minute.

'Lots of nice whitewash on the rocks. Are you seeing anything?'

It was pretty up there at the top of the glen, sunshine still bathing the curving ridges and hillsides to the east, highlighting the quartz on granite boulders so that they glinted and sparkled in early evening brilliance. Fresh green foliage of oak, rowan and birch fluttered in the breeze and the dark heather moor beyond shimmered in the dying heat of the day. Shadows were already creeping over the flanks of the west ridge and its cliffs and gullies were shrouded in gloom.

'Only the inanimate beauties of nature,' I mocked.

But was that right? Remains of old woods dotted the hillside below the corrie and in the gullies of two burns which slit its sides alder and willow grew thick. Plenty of cover for red deer. I suddenly noticed they were there, a small group of hinds, moving out of the trees and into a clearing, ten of them, and four young calves no more than a few days old. Several of the hinds looked heavily pregnant as if their young would soon be born. Summer rust-red coats were polished bright in the sunshine and short tails and sensitive ears flicked impatiently with the torment of midges and flies.

'Do you see them?' exclaimed Don suddenly.

I thought he meant the deer. 'Sure. Only a few calves yet.'

'Not calves, idiot. Eagles!'

Ah! Forgetting the hinds at once, I looked higher into a deep blue sky where puff balls of cumulus were forming. Two eagles were gliding there, tawny feathers glowing, wings with primaries spread, translucent in the brilliant light. They floated lazily round and round on the somnolent air, hide and seek in the cloud, a dip of a wing here, a rudder tail compensating there, hardly working at all and apparently enjoying the perfect evening.

'They're beautiful!' I exclaimed, finding it necessary to state the obvious. 'What do you think they're up to?'

'Just enjoying a break from parental duties, probably,' Don suggested, laughing.

'Who wouldn't?' I countered.

Although there appeared to be no special purpose in their flying, both eagles were in fact sinking lower over the glen. They glided round and round in ever-diminishing circles as if perhaps planning to land on a rock or a branch to rest. Or maybe they were now on their way back to the eyrie. The former was possible but the latter unlikely – their flight then would have been more purposeful, a low sweeping in towards the cliff, a merging with its dark background and, finally, an alighting on its ledge unobtrusively and probably unseen. Floating in and out of sunshine and shade against sun-dappled hillsides, it looked as though the great birds now had something else in mind.

The majestic pair, wings hardly moving, tails bending lazily from side to side, hooked bills sharply etched against a puff-ball cloud, had their heads down.

'Do you think they're after the deer?' I asked Don.

'Maybe. They might tease them a little. Nothing serious.'

'The hinds are not very happy,' I suggested.

They were certainly beginning to be uneasy. Some stopped feeding and instead watched the eagles anxiously. Sensing concern, their young stood close by, puzzled but not yet frightened. The group leader, an old and experienced matriarch, did not seem unduly worried. Jaws still working on a mouthful, she gave the great birds a casual glance from time to time but showed no signs of panic.

There may have been a warning call from her, however, which of course we could not hear. For suddenly, dramatically, the mood changed. The calves all began scurrying for their mothers and, safely sorted out, each to its own, were nuzzling into their bellies for reassurance. Every adult head was raised to the eagles as they sank lower and lower. Almost at once, the great birds were hovering only a hundred feet or so above the deer, like enormous buzzards. Wings outstretched, heads down and talons flexed, they watched and waited, apparently looking for the moment to pounce. As the endless moments dragged by, prolonging the suspense, it looked as if they could hang on the air for ever.

Golden eagles often harass deer in this fashion, usually by stooping again and again over their heads, teasing them until their nerves snap and they take fright. The birds are just practising the skills of hunting, and we had so far never seen a kill. Usually they grew tired of the game, and flew off upon other business.

'I think they *are* serious this time,' I murmured, as the excitement began to grip.

The drama continued for several minutes more, eagles hovering, deer undecided. Then the moment arrived. Two golden birds came swooping, wings tight, feathers ruffling, the hen leading, her smaller mate tucked in behind, both hurtling down as if to a certain death. Just as it seemed they must crash into the deer, they swerved away with split-second timing and were effortlessly soaring upwards. As they climbed insolently into the heavens, they seemed to be mocking the deer: look out, we're not finished with you yet.

Still the deer held their ground, perhaps waiting to see if the eagles meant serious business. Neither chewing cud nor grazing, they stood alert and quite still, heads raised to the sky watching the golden birds. When those magnificent creatures of the air came plunging down once more, feathers aflame in the last of the sunshine, the matriarch at last gave way. With forelegs digging deep to gain momentum, hindlegs kicking hard, she turned and fled.

All the deer panicked. Away they bolted, apparently terrified, knees lifting high, burnt-brown bodies stretching long and low over boulders, bushy heather, and ditches we could not see, matchlessly beautiful in their headlong flight. The little calves, obedient and perhaps sensing fear, set off after their mothers, trying desperately to catch up but all the while falling farther and farther behind. The adults ignored them, neither slowing down nor stopping to wait. As the eagles came again and again, banking away with consummate ease at each heart-stopping last moment, the hinds gathered speed, quite forgetting their young. Safety would be in a small, thickly-wooded area at the top of the glen, and towards that they seemed to be fleeing.

'There's a little one not going to make it,' I said, totally absorbed in the drama and suddenly noticing a small straggler.

'Afraid so,' Don replied.

One of the calves, probably only a few days old, was falling well behind the others. It kept stumbling on the rough, rutted ground, running then walking, pausing a moment to rest, then staggering on, blindly following the instinct to be with the herd and stay alive.

'I think the eagles know it,' said Don. 'They mean business all right.'

'Poor little thing,' I could not help saying.

Highland landscape, remnant of the ancient pine forest

Fox cubs out of the den and into a new world

Fox cubs await parents' return with prey

Alert young fox cub

Rusty tries a new home, watched by Shuna

Venturing out and about

Shian nursing Rufus on the sofa

Rufus growing up

The hunters had now changed tactics. Perhaps sensing a kill they no longer harried the hinds, who were still in headlong flight, but were now hovering on fast-flapping wings over the struggling creature. And, as the little calf lurched across the rough hillside towards its inevitable end, my feelings were mixed – difficult not to pity the poor thing, so small and vulnerable, but fascinating to watch an event never seen before. I hoped we would indeed see the ending.

The calf came at last to a boisterous burn which, in spate from recent rain, was tumbling headlong down the hillside. From afar we could see white water frothing and bubbling over the boulders in its bed. It was quite broad, too, at this point. Gamely the little one tried to leap over, could not make the distance, and appeared to collapse in a heap. From a distance, and through binoculars, it looked as if it was caught, helpless, between two boulders and was too weak to free itself. In a little while we saw its head sink back and hoped it drowned quickly.

The eagles came gliding down towards the burn, in no hurry now. They landed close beside their victim and, possession established, began nonchalantly to preen, streaking through breast and back feathers with fearsome, efficient bills and appearing to be quite uninterested in their prey. Then the hen took off, climbing easily into the evening air, soaring on the northerly breeze and twice circling round over her mate. She glided in towards the eyrie cliff and disappeared somewhere in its shadowed gloom. The cock hopped clumsily off his perch on a rock, strutted solemnly the few feet to the bank, then with an ungainly leap and outstretched talons landed on the side of his prey. We watched him struggle to lift the small spotted creature from the water then drop it in a nearby patch of heather. He took off once more, and appeared to be following his mate towards the cliff.

'What's he up to?' I exclaimed in surprise.

'He'll come back when he's hungry,' Don assured me. 'But I don't think we can wait. We need to get up to the den before the light goes.'

'There is also the small matter of the tent,' I agreed.

Now began the tough part of the journey, the climb towards the cliffs of the eagle eyrie. It was a trip often made before, no trail to be blazed, but with heavy packs slower going than usual.

We took it steadily with many a stop for a breather. The burn was crossed much higher up where it was narrower and there were stepping-stone rocks. Then it was fairly easy going through birch and oak on a steep hillside scattered with rock. When we reached the heather we could follow tracks made by sheep and deer and these took us into a steep gully which broke the hillside some way to the left of the eagle cliff. Here a trickling burn from the watershed above had become a mighty waterfall, crashing through the boulders and casting a fine mist over the heather and rock on either side. It was pleasantly cool after the climb and out of the sun.

There had been no sign of the eagles all this time but we knew that at least one of them would have watched our progress every inch of the way up the hillside. These birds are easily scared by human presence. In April, when we first check for signs of refurbishing of the nest, and later, during the early stages of nesting, we never go near the eyries at all but use a telescope to see what is going on. Though we were nowhere near it right now, and in any case it was most unlikely the hen would desert her chicks at this stage, we were taking no chances and slid into the cover of the gully as quickly as possible.

'I'll just nip over to the hide and see what's going on,' said Don. 'You get the tent up.'

'Okay,' I agreed, a trifle reluctantly as I would have liked to go and look at the eyrie as well. But Don's suggestion made sense.

The hide was a permanent one, repaired each winter in case the eagles used that particular eyrie the following season. The camp site, on the other hand, was a narrow ledge right beside the waterfall, built up with turf and heather branches. It was the only available spot for a tent, which of course had to be erected each time it was needed, and that was a distinctly tricky operation. All being well at the fox den, it would be late when we returned, and dark.

Don was not away long. I was just dumping the gear under cover when he returned.

'Two chicks.' He smiled as he scrambled down the rocky side of the gully. 'They're probably four to five weeks old and doing fine.'

'Any sign of the adults?' I asked.

'No. I expect they saw us disappear and then lost interest.

They'll probably pick us up again as we go to the den.'

As indeed they did. To avoid disturbing the eagles we climbed right to the top of the gully and then made the easy walk, as fast as possible, along the heather-covered ridge which was well behind their cliff. This would bring us to a place high above the den from which we could recce for the vixen, or dog, that might just be quartering the hillside somewhere below. When we arrived, however, there was nothing to be seen and we made our way quickly down. As we slipped into the hiding place we always used when the wind was from the north, we turned briefly to look towards the eagle cliffs. And there she was. A golden eagle, as expected, silhouetted against a pale sky, and surely the hen. She was gliding in towards the eyrie, and we felt sure she had been keeping an eye on us and now was home for the night to brood her family.

With a quick look through binoculars, it was pleasing to discover the familiar evidence of an occupied den. The soil in front of the entrance was bare and worn down, the ground all around well padded. The vegetation was trampled and even a bank of blaeberry had been flattened by rampaging feet. The heather farther out was threaded by narrow paths all homing in on the den, but as far as we could see there were no satellite holes, though they could have been hidden in a clump of bracken. Undoubtedly, here was a much-used place and there must surely be cubs. We breathed a sigh of relief.

By now the sun had vanished behind the higher hills to the west and movement in the air had died away. Midges were at work. The sky was a playground for pink and gold puff balls, banking ahead of heavenly breezes and building to giant castles in a pale incandescent void. The cliffs of the corrie basked in reflected light and ferns and grasses were green relief against their harsh sides. Scree from the top was a fall of flame cascading to a shadowed bottom, and immense boulders, in the gloom of dusk already arrived there, were mysterious presences ready to conceal the secrets of the night. As we knew it would be, the whole area around the den was still bathed in the residual light of evening. It glowed pink and gold in soft radiance and seemed to await a great drama.

It was, in fact, business as usual for the foxes and a scene we had often witnessed before. It had been a hot day, roasting for young cubs confined to the den, and they would be eager to cool off. Very soon, one came scampering out followed closely by another, then one more cautious, taking its time, testing the air with an enquiring nose. Another two arrived, still yawning and probably following the others because it was instinctive to do so.

'They're not as big as Rufus and Rusty,' I whispered.

'Mm,' replied Don. 'About the same age I should think. Probably not as well fed.'

'We should have some fun anyway,' I added, thinking of the usual games that young foxes get up to.

This lot, however, were not in playful mood at the moment. They were hungry. One flew straight for a nearby bone and when another charged over to challenge it they scrapped for a minute, snapping and snarling with teeth bared, holding on for dear life but getting nowhere, angling all the while for a position of strength from which the prize could be pulled away. They finished up, each on an end of the bone, grimly holding on and butting each other with their haunches. Eventually growing tired, one of them let go and sauntered off with a swagger, as if to say 'it's a rotten bone anyway'. We decided both these cubs were probably males.

Meanwhile another big chap, about the same size, was nosing around among the boulders. He found a piece of what, from a distance and through binoculars, looked like the skin of a hare. He chewed energetically for a moment or two, evidently found it unappetising, then ran over to dispute the bone. The dominant cub presented his rear end to his sibling, making it quite clear whose bone it was, and he slunk away. Numbers four and five were sitting companionably together scratching their coats and yawning sleep away. We decided – and really it was just guesswork – that they were little females. Certainly they were quite a bit smaller and did not seem so competitive. All five cubs had white tips to their tails.

Number three cub was now making his way along a little path in the heather. He was slinking there just like a grown-up fox might do, head down to the trail and nosing into the heather on either side. Suddenly he froze, a small presence sitting bolt upright, ears pricked forward and eyes glued, all petrified attention. The moment arrived. Gathering his haunches together, he hesitated, then leapt. Plonk, he pounced, and missed. His head came up with nothing in his jaws and he stood looking puzzled, staring at the spot as if he could not believe his eyes: surely there had been something there! He began sniffing the ground again and two other cubs came running to join him. Then all three were industriously nosing about in the vegetation and scraping it furiously this way and that. Maybe they already knew all about voles.

'Looks as though they've been hunting with mum,' chuckled Don.

'It's interesting to think that Rufus and Rusty are already doing the same but with no mum to teach them,' I remarked. 'Perhaps it's all instinctive.'

Unsuccessful vole hunting soon proving unpopular, the cubs began a rumbustious romp. The two females joined in and we watched five beautiful tawny young creatures all tearing in and out of the bracken, rudely parting and breaking its stems, leaping over the heather and into the blaeberry patch, each apparently trying to catch the one immediately in front. Number one fell over on to his back and they all muscled in – a confusion of snapping, snarling, squealing, kicking, leaping and pouncing youngsters. The cliff-like sides of the corrie were baffle-board amplifiers, and all the world must hear them.

'That should bring a parent,' I whispered to Don, as we listened to the uninhibited squeals and shrieks.

He had hardly nodded when the vixen did indeed appear. Not from a hunting trip, as we had guessed, but from within the den. If she had been enjoying a few moments' peace without her family then the noise they were making now would have roused the dead. The two smallest cubs came running to her at once submissively crouching low and wagging their tails. No doubt friendly chirruping sounds were being uttered as well, but we could not hear them at that distance. The three big ones broke off their game momentarily to see what was happening – three youngsters all attention, ears pricked and heads turned to their mother. They must have realised, at once, that she had not brought food, so they began romping again. The soft call she would have given could not be heard, but there must have been one. Suddenly the newly started game stopped abruptly, the cubs scampered to join their mother, and the whole family vanished down into the den.

'Let's see if the dog brings food,' suggested Don. 'There's light enough yet.'

'Just!' I agreed.

This experience at dusk never loses its fascination – light fading, colour vanishing, and dark shadows spreading over the corrie, making its rocky sides and scattered boulders seem larger and more menacing than they really are. It is infinitely mysterious, and you become tense with expectation that something exciting will surely happen. Colour is a memory only, actuality greyness fading slowly into impenetrable blackness. As eyes become useless, ears strain to pick up tiny sounds that are clues to action out there in the night. Imagination takes over. Is that a stealthy creature creeping through the rocks? What could be rustling the vegetation over there? Is that little twittering sound a friendly cub talking to another or a small bird settling to roost with its mates on a nearby perch? And so on.

The last of the breeze had died by now and it was utterly still. We began to worry that the dog, if he came at all, would pick up our scent, for foxes have amazing scenting powers and we had no idea from which direction he would come. We waited, and waited, watching all residual light inexorably fading and feeling reasonably sure that if only it could last we would see action. With binoculars you can often pick up detail in darkness that the eye, unaided, cannot but the trouble is you need some sort of clue, a tiny movement caught or a small sound, in order to pinpoint it. This time we were lucky. Only a few minutes later, when we had almost given up hope, the white tip of a bushy tail appeared in the gloaming and binoculars identified a shadowy form. It was certainly a fox. It could be the dog.

We lost the creature, then found it again, and as it climbed steadily higher saw more clearly a slinking shape, long-bodied, creeping slowly through the vegetation, disappearing occasionally behind a boulder and giving us a heart attack in case we had lost it, stopping from time to time to sniff the air. It came, at last, to a paler patch of well-trampled grass a little way down the corrie and directly below the den. Against this background we could now see our fox clearly. It was a large animal. It had a hare in its jaws. It was getting closer to the den. Surely, it must be the dog.

About five yards from the den the dog fox came to a halt. The hare was dropped and then he probably uttered that curiously inviting chirrup which foxes always seem to use when bringing food for the family. The vixen, eager and hungry, came running to meet him. There were no greetings. She rudely snatched the hare, shook it into her jaws and made straight back towards the den. We missed her call to the cubs but could just pick out in the gathering darkness a mêlée of movement at the entrance. No doubt cubs were squabbling over a meal. We could easily hear their excited squealing. The dog, used to the performance but on this occasion having no contact with his family, turned away and stalked back into the cover of the night. He would probably curl up somewhere in the bracken to have a spell before setting off again to hunt. The vixen, too, seemed to have disappeared. Perhaps, with her family happily feeding, she had joined her mate.

Soon there was no possibility of seeing anything, even through binoculars. We crept as quietly as possible and extremely slowly over the rough terrain up the hillside and then, more quickly, back along the ridge. Hazards were boulders we seemed never to have noticed before and trails followed through the heather that did not, after all, go where they should have done. An hour later the little tent was a welcome orange glow in the darkness and a cup of tea went down well.

We neither slid away down the hillside during the night nor were drowned by the waterfall and the sound of its thundering conveniently woke us at 3 a.m., the moment we wanted. It was still as dark as it ever would be on a short June night in the Highlands. Normally we would both arrive at a hide and once one had entered the other would depart. Assuming that birds cannot count, the intruders would thus have been seen to disappear from the scene and the bird at the nest would not be disturbed. On this occasion, because time was short and Rufus and Rusty should not be left for too much longer, we planned to enter the eagle hide together. Under cover of darkness and in the shadow of the great cliff, there was little risk of upsetting the birds.

It was a delicate operation and could only have been done with intimate knowledge of the ground to be covered. The glen below seemed a remote faraway place, sensed rather than seen, but the immediate surroundings were a nebulous wilderness of pebbles which must not be dislodged and vegetation which must not be rustled. The ridge away to the east was etched sharply against a translucent sky awaiting the sun, but behind us it was still shadowed and dark. A ghostly silence hung over all and as we crept carefully along, tiny sounds seemed magnified a hundred times to echo loud and clear over the hillside.

At last we squeezed through the small entrance hole at the back of the hide and froze to listen for trouble. There was none. No murmurings came from the animal world out there. No shape could be identified on the eyrie, no stirrings or sounds that suggested eagles disturbed, or even about to start their day. We settled as quietly as possible into a bed of old bracken to await the inevitable onslaught of midges and the thrilling happenings which would make it all worthwhile. The silence seemed almost tangible, a velvet cloak that enveloped our secret hiding place, a curtain which soon would be parted upon the first breathless moments of the day to reveal the private life of an eagle family. I wished we could be a part of that silence, out in it, camouflaged by its dark concealing folds, able to watch, undetected, all the creatures start their day.

At five o'clock the sun, a throbbing golden orb, rose out of a fiery bed and climbed above the opposite ridge. From the birches below a broken-voiced cuckoo, announcing its predatory presence, spoke good-morning to all small birds in the vicinity. A mountain blackbird scolded sharply, the sound lifting from one perch and then another as it made its way slowly across the hillside. As if prompted by these peremptory calls to action, larks, pipits and wheatears all began their morning songs. A spotted woodpecker in the wood below hammered a message to its mate. Seen through our peepholes the eagle eyrie was revealed in all its glory, its supporting ledge, only minutes ago a place of mystery, now bathed in warm golden light. Against a backdrop of rock glistening with sparkling dew-drops, the huge dark pile of sticks seemed a suitably impressive home for two majestic birds. Built up over many years, it was probably six feet in diameter, three or four feet in depth, and might have weighed several hundred-weights.

To complete this breath-taking moment, a presence serene and silent stood motionless there. The golden eagle hen. Her tawny feathers glowed in the light of the risen sun and her head was a rich chestnut brown.

With dismay, I suddenly realised this glorious bird was staring straight at the hide! Had she, with her superlative eagle eyesight, spotted us through the tiny peepholes? Or had she heard sounds that puzzled her? It was a bad moment. Discovery would mean the end of eagle watching and, at once, an ostentatious departure down the hillside so that she knew we had gone. But then, as a small bird whistled softly nearby, the piercing eyes swivelled away from the hide and became instantly focused on something else. Two tiny wrens had caught her attention. With cheeky upturned tails, they were flitting boldly about on the sticks at the edge of the eyrie, twittering companionably together as they caught insect breakfasts from the decaying flesh of eagle prey, and appeared totally unaware of the huge bird towering above, watching their antics.

The little birds must have served us well for it seemed the eagle hen had forgotten the hide. In a minute, evidently tired of the wrens, she stalked back to the centre of the nest, made herself comfortable with much fidgeting of feather-plusfoured legs and mantling of great wings over her chicks, then wearily closed her eyes. We could not help smiling at the look of utter resignation on her face: another boring duty to be performed!

The nest certainly looked well-used. Whitewash bespattered the perimeter sticks and cascaded down the rockface below. The centre was well trodden and the shelf beyond littered with the bleached bones of discarded prey. The inevitable piece of rowan, seemingly daintily arranged, probably by the hen, shone green and fresh against the dark pile of sticks, proclaiming that this was indeed a home in use. Decorating the nest in this fashion seems to be a universal habit of eagles, but the reason for it is not clear. It happens each breeding season and is quite deliberate.

The hen was not allowed to rest for long. In a few minutes, her eyes still closed, there came small stirrings from under her protecting wings, which turned immediately into a miniature earthquake. A small eaglet head, ruffled and downy, poked through her soft feathering and was followed immediately by the rest of an untidy, pepper-and-salt body. It shook itself vigorously in a flurry of feathers and powder-puff down, yawned, then stood uncertainly beside its mother blinking in the sunshine. One chick. Another eruption of down and feathers and a second was soon yawning beside its sibling.

Brooding duties over, the hen began shaking out her feathers and picking with her fearsome bill at her breast. It was a brief toilet. In only a few moments she stalked to the edge of the eyrie, stood a moment assessing the misty glen below, then launched herself effortlessly into the stillness of the morning. We watched her floating on long, barely moving wings towards the farther ridge, then lost sight of her. She probably alighted somewhere on the hillside to await her mate.

'We're in luck at last,' I whispered gleefully, able to speak quietly now the hen was away.

I meant, of course, thank goodness that they are all safe. Unfortunately there are greedy, or thoughtless, folk who for money, or just to feel good in outwitting authority, steal the eggs of birds which are on the list of protected species. The golden eagle is, of course, one of these. Sometimes the young are taken. It is impossible to have every eyrie closely guarded twenty-four hours a day for every day of the breeding season, so we often experience anger and sadness when watching frustrated eagle parents flying aimlessly around the cliffs of their nesting site, or perching for hours on the hillside, with no family to raise and therefore none of the routine tasks of brooding, caring and hunting to be done.

Left to themselves, the chicks began to tramp around the nest with enormous feet, strangely out of proportion to the rest of their small bodies, stumbling over the sticks and poking in among them for something to eat. In a desultory sort of fashion they tore at pieces of raw flesh, the flies rising from each bloody morsel to buzz angrily round their heads. They were not really hungry and soon grew bored, beginning to preen instead. Small bills industriously darted in and out of speckled black-and-white breasts, picking out soft down and smoothing feathers into place. Each piece of fluff was solemnly observed as it floated downwards to the sticks, feather cleaning not resumed until it had safely landed.

Wing-strengthening exercises then replaced this careful toilet, energetic jumping up and down, lifting high and dangerously off the sticks so that we wondered if they could possibly land safely again. Wings working harder with every attempt, each leap became a fragment of time when the birds were airborne, their landing a precarious wobble. Not surprisingly, they soon grew

tired – take-off day was still a long way ahead for these youngsters. All at once, they were treading awkwardly over the sticks
into the hollow of the nest and collapsing into its depths. The
regular rising and falling of the feathers on their backs told us
they were instantly asleep.

'One is already a bit larger than the other,' I remarked. 'Do
you think it's a female?'

'Could be,' Don replied. 'Or it is the greedier and dominant
of two of the same sex. Did you see that gash on the head of the
smaller one?'

'It didn't look too bad. Perhaps it's a "toughy". It would be great
if they both survive.'

So often, when there are two chicks, only one lives to fly the
nest. The dominant sibling grabs most of the food and bullies
the other unmercifully until, at last, from ceaseless pecking and
starvation it dies. The reason is not clear, and it often happens
even where there is no shortage of prey. Perhaps this one would
be an exception.

It was becoming warm now in the hide and I regretted the
thermos of tea I had been too lazy to make. We eased cramped
limbs and tried not to rustle the dead foliage beneath us. Half an
hour passed and the sun was now well above the ridge. Pockets
of mist chased each other up the hillside to vanish into blue
emptiness above and the glen was taking on brilliant colour, its
greenery fresh and glittering with early morning dew.

All of a sudden, and for no obvious reason, the young eaglets
came to life. Both heads were lifted and they began to cheep
expectantly, tentatively at first but quickly turning plaintive and
more and more urgent. There came a familiar tingling down my
spine, and then, immediately, that soft swishing sound as air
passed through the primary feathers of a great bird. The cock
alighted on the edge of the eyrie. He stood, quite motionless,
looking back into the wide expanse of the glen and taking no
notice at all of the chicks that were jumping up and down with
excitement. Bills agape, they kept pressing towards him, but he
had brought them nothing. All his attention seemed to be fixed
on something more interesting.

The youngsters settled with resignation into their nesting
hollow, a routine reaction when no offerings were presented, and
we had a good opportunity to look at the adult. A smaller version

of his mate, he appeared to be a deeper chestnut, but that may have been an effect of the sunshine which now enfolded the eyrie in warm light. With haughty stare, and quite unaware of two people close by admiring his superb self, the cock was totally absorbed with something on the opposite hillside. Suddenly, as his head tilted yet again to one side, we realised he was listening as well as looking. Then we heard the curious strangled yelp that eagles sometimes use to communicate with each other – a call rather similar to a collie dog's yap when speaking sharply to a recalcitrant ewe. Almost at once the cock replied.

We held our breath, shrinking – if it were possible – farther into the dark recesses of the hide. Then there was a flurry in the air and the hen, a large bundle of fur in her talons, alighted most ungracefully on the edge of the eyrie. She wobbled a moment, off-balance, but kept one foot still firmly holding her prey. I gasped. No wonder she was a little clumsy. It was the haunch of a red deer calf that she had brought in. I thought of the kill of yesterday and glanced towards Don. He acknowledged the silent question with a smile and a thumbs-up signal. It seemed likely that one of the pair had carried the dead calf to a place quite close to the eyrie and the carcase would satisfy the needs of the whole family for a little while.

The chicks came charging towards their mother, blundering over the sticks and clamouring loudly to be fed. She tore off a piece and presented it, the larger chick darting a savage bill at its sibling and rudely barging it out of the way, greedily seizing, swallowing and demanding more. The smaller chick subsided submissively into the nest, but the cock came strutting to its rescue. He too tore a piece from the haunch, held it in his bill for a moment and then neatly presented it. The offering was ravenously accepted. And so it continued for several minutes, two golden eagles, heads down and tails up, a gentle breeze ruffling the feathers on their rumps, tearing with fearsome bills at the bloody mess and daintily presenting small scraps to their chicks with a sideways motion of the head. We watched enchanted, for though we had occasionally seen two eagle parents on the nest at the same moment, usually at changeover time for brooding duties, we had never before seen them together feeding their young.

The eaglets were quickly satisfied. One second they were each gaping hungrily for a mouthful, the next they had lost interest and were standing by lazily picking at the down on their breasts. Parental duties over, the two golden adults fed themselves. There was nothing dainty about that either, each mouthful being efficiently and quickly torn from a carcase held in place with sharp talons and golloped down with all possible haste.

The cock finished feeding first. He stood idly looking around as if uncertain what he might do next, then stalked solemnly to the edge of the eyrie, turned himself round, and ejected an impressive white stream to further decorate the cliff below. Feeling better perhaps, and facing out once more, he stood for a moment on the perimeter sticks, apparently regarding the glen below, then floated easily away on six-foot-span wings. Without a glance at her family, the hen followed almost immediately. We watched them, from peepholes at the back of the hide, gliding over the glen and landing, each on a rock, high on the opposite hillside. There they began to preen.

Very soon the chicks were yawning, subsiding back into the hollow of their nest and once more falling fast asleep. The eyrie would be sheltered from the sun, when later in the morning it grew very warm, by a broad overhang of rock and a small rowan tree growing out of a cleft beside it. As we watched the satisfied youngsters doing what all small creatures do after a feed, there came a gentle 'baa' from somewhere below our rock. I looked down. There, directly beneath the eyrie shelf, some thirty to forty feet below, an old ewe was quietly grazing on a patch of grass, her lamb contentedly at her side. A few feet away a hind was suckling her calf. Don reported that neither of the mothers had even lifted her head as the eagles flew over. So much for the wicked ways of these predatory birds.

'I think we should leave as soon as possible,' Don said.

'The adults won't return for a while now the chicks are fed,' I agreed.

'There's plenty on the eyrie, anyway.'

'And Rufus and Rusty will be looking for us.'

Our charges back home had been forgotten in the excitement of the last few hours.

'Let's wait a few minutes,' Don suggested. 'The adults will probably go off hunting and it would be better if they don't see us leave the hide.'

Soon we saw first the hen, then the cock, take off from their perches and rise easily to a great height. They flew north and would soon pass out of sight over a ridge. It was most unlikely they would spot two objects crawling from the hide, sticking closely to the cliff and making their way round the back of the hill to the tent. Not much later, laden with all the gear, we were scrambling down the waterfall gully to the burn in the bottom of the glen and following its track to the five tall pines at its entrance. We would return again to see how our fox and eagle families were doing.

THREE

Death on the Moor

THE HIGHLAND HILLSIDE is dappled in sunshine and shade. Majestic pine, graceful birch, sturdy rowan and fluttering aspen all mantle its slopes and reach long green fingers towards rugged rock ridges and peaks. Breezes sigh softly through the ladies of the wood shivering their silver green foliage. Stems of ancient pine glow warmest pink in the sunshine and climb straight, and crooked too, towards dark and swaying canopies. Whispering winds bend their branches to creaking protest. Slender needles of pine thickly litter the woodland floor and yellowed islands in their midst are the fallen leaves, dying and dead, of birch.

I dream on. The woods are alive with birds. Black, brown, grey, blue, green, yellow and red feathering in spring and summer is the bright attraction, or drab disguise, of its inhabitants. Territorial song fills the air with urgent sound. The capercaillie cock, king of forest birds, click-calls softly from high in pine branches, then with outspread wings floats down to his chosen lekking place. He struts haughtily up and down, a pompous gentleman who fans black, green, purple, brown and grey feathering and leaps six tremendous feet in the air when excitement reaches its peak. His song is the liquid gurgling of a bottle being poured and the explosive hiss of champagne when the cork is pulled. In clearings among the birch blackcock croon pianissimo in the dawn, their bubblings and croodlings rising to frenzied fortissimo as dominant males battle for the finest of the hens.

The warning squawks of a hoodie crow echo suddenly through

the forest, instantly silencing the harmonious warblings of little birds. A goshawk floats smoothly by, weaving in and out of tree-top shadowed space, hawk-eye searching for prey – the scream of a careless young blackbird shatters the silence and the predator has struck. The bird is carried in his foot to a favourite stump and there he plucks it, tearing the feathers out in beakfuls and dropping them, haphazardly, to the ground. Nearby, on an untidy nest of sticks high in a pine, his mate has four chicks. They need to be fed and she waits impatiently to collect his offering.

Not far away a fox pads businesslike through the trees, off to a place he knows of where voles are plentiful. From a hole in the trunk of an old pine a polecat turns briefly to watch him, then plunges with a vole in her mouth to kits in snug depths below. On the branch of a nearby pine a lynx rests long and lean, tail twitching lazily, slit eyes assessing, tufted ears erect and listening. It notes the passing of these lesser beings but is not concerned – its belly is comfortably full and it will doze.

From high on the hill in the early morning, a wolf lifts his voice to the heavens, vibrant, haunting, ominous, calling to his mate at her den. The reply is immediate and soon the aroused woodland is filled with the melancholy messages of a family of wolves planning to hunt. Up there, on bare cliff ledges, jackdaws stir and begin the gossiping and quarrelling of the day. Below, in the forest, red deer stir uneasily, noting the eerie wolf-sound and lifting sensitive noses to the air.

A golden eagle in a cloudless sky speaks a mewing message to its mate. Speaks? Spoke? I started from my fantasy of another time and awoke to reality: a pair of eagles calling from out of the blue above, and the pathetic remnant of a once impressive wood through which we were passing. As I had walked slowly along in the soft light of early morning it had been the melancholy evidence around me that had set me dreaming of that ancient Wood of Caledon: straggling roots of grand old trees long dead, now held fast in long ago laid down peat; dismal scatterings of descendant pine and birch still clinging to life, but slowly dying; no young saplings sprouting tall and straight to become the wood of the future; a woodland disaster surely the responsibility of man. To a forester it was a nightmare, a place that once was magic and now was fast decaying into oblivion.

Eagle calls came again. The Eagle Glen was not too far away, no distance at all for these great birds. Perhaps they were joyfully stretching their wings on early morning breezes up there before flying off to hunt. Distant movement among the trees ahead caught my eye and six hinds, not too much alarmed by our approach but thinking it better to go, stepped daintily up a narrow path through the heather towards the open hill – a trail long since blazed by their ancestors, they would go no other way. I hurried to catch up with Don who was walking fast. Though mourning the passing of an old wood, he would have been entirely in the present with plans for the day in mind, and the need to get on with a job.

'I was nearly coming back to look for you,' he joked, knowing I was always tempted to linger in this place.

'It's heart-breaking,' I sighed.

'I hope someone will do something about these old woods one day.'

'What could be done?' I asked.

'Well, for a start they could be fenced to keep out the sheep and deer.'

'That would be very expensive, wouldn't it?'

'Worth it, though. These remnants should be a national heritage and also a nursery for the future.'

Trees are an important part of our philosophy, but today we were on our way to look at the nest of a hen harrier. Back in May we had watched the spectacular displaying of a courting pair over the moor which stretched for miles beyond the old wood. Two birds had been soaring steeply after each other into an azure sky, rolling languidly over to stoop swiftly, then swooping up and over again, again and again. They had continued their spectacular aerobatics in joyous abandon for many minutes, totally engrossed with one another and completely unconscious of two admiring spectators below. Then, a climax reached, or both ready, they had come hurtling down towards the heather, levelling out with insolent ease and planing low to the place they had chosen. Both dropped out of sight, and we imagined their mating and noted the spot, for there the hen would probably nest.

A few weeks later we had come slowly through the heather, talking softly all the while to alert the hen of our approach. A tranquil bird, nicely camouflaged with her surroundings, she had been reluctant to leave her eggs. We were within yards before she rose, without protest, to climb high into the sky above our heads. There she proceeded to circle round and round, head down, watching what we would do but making no attempt to harass us. Only a few more careful steps and there was the nest, a hollow in the heather, lined with molinia grass and nicely sheltered from the worst of the weather. A clutch of five blue-white eggs glinted palely in the centre, and for a moment or two we stood admiring them. Then we quickly laid the foundations of what would eventually become a hide, leaving its poles in a pile on a selected spot and placing a few bundles of heather in among them. Then we took ourselves off.

From a thicket of gorse some distance away we had waited anxiously to see what the hen would do. Would she return to her nest? She did. Almost as soon as we were more or less concealed, she had come quickly gliding back, unruffled, to her eggs. The 'bush' which had mysteriously grown in her absence (Don's hide) did not appear to worry her. She scarcely gave it a glance. We left shortly after, reassured she was safely settled and planning a photography session with the family later on. That was several weeks, and several visits, ago in order gradually to build up the hide. Now, as we passed out of the shadowy old pine wood, we took a quick look through binoculars to see what birds were about and to pinpoint a small white rag tied to a heather branch, the marker for the nest. At the moment, no harriers; but the rag was still bravely there, limply stirring in the tiny breeze.

It promised to be a lovely day. Heather carpeted most of the area and outcrops of rock, in patches bare of vegetation, were shimmering desert islands in the risen sun. A ridge of higher ground, dawn mist still climbing its sides, broke the skyline to the north and was impressively back-dropped by peaks in the distance. Its craggy length was split in two by a gully, and an eroding burn, impetuous in times of rainfall, gentle in drought, was gradually wearing away its rock, moulding it, scoring it and grinding it to silt. The gully was strewn with large boulders. Meeting the moor, the burn meandered a short way through the heather, then ended its journey in a small lochan. The mist hung over the waters there, but its curtains were gradually parting to the sun to reveal glittering, rippling pools of light. A mallard mother was leading her flotilla flock in and out of cottonwool cover towards a small island. There she had probably nested.

Further to the east was complete contrast. Forest modernity climbed a long, gentle rise and vanished out of sight over the ridge. Douglas fir, spruce, larch and pine were young trees as yet, giving an overwhelming impression of a plantation, ordered ranks and regular rides, the artificial work of man. Alien, awkward contrast to the moor and the old wood we had just left behind, no one would think it beautiful. But Don, with his forestry training, could see a future when it would become a gracious and pleasing place – no clear-felling then, but a gradual thinning of the trees when the time was right, and the remainder allowed to grow on to maturity. At present though, and for some time to come, it was excellent habitat for small birds and mammals, and these would be prey for the hen harrier pair and enable them to raise a family. In fact, pausing to look through binoculars once again, we glimpsed a slim grey bird with streamlined, black-tipped wings and a head with the bill of a hawk. It was a cock hen harrier and he was chasing a small bird in and out of the young trees. A short-eared owl was hunting low over the trees, too, sharp-eyed for movement of an unwary vole.

'He's busy anyway,' Don said with satisfaction, referring to the harrier. 'Sure to have a family!'

'You never know,' I quipped. 'Perhaps he's just hunting for his own dinner.'

'Any sign of the hen?'

'She'll be with the chicks, surely.'

'Hope so.'

Until we actually see the evidence that all is well we tend to imagine the worst: a nest destroyed by gamekeepers or violated by some predator or other. There were no obvious signs of disaster, however, so we tramped slowly towards the nest, rustling through the heather and taking no trouble to disguise our approach. In due course, and while we were still some distance away, she rose quietly into the air and with no fuss or noisy objection flapped off across the moor. Good. All should be well.

'Not much wrong with that lot,' Don remarked as we stood gazing down at a nest all higgledy-piggledy, the heather trampled and bespattered with 'white-wash'.

'Comic characters,' was my comment as we took in three

speckled youngsters well on the way to adult feathering and two fluffy balls still in grey down. Small dark eyes twinkled in the sunshine and their bills were expectantly agape: feed us. Three were large and obviously winning the major share of the food brought in by the parents, the remaining two almost puny, though one was a little bigger than the other.

Hen harrier eggs are laid over a period of about a week and the chicks hatch off to match. Thus by the time the last has pecked its way into existence, its siblings, in asynchronous order, have had a head start in their growth and development. When all are hatched, the dominant birds will be the ones to grab the available feeding and if there is a shortage, the smaller and weaker will go without – eventually they may die and be eaten by the others. If the shortage of food is such that there is insufficient to keep even one chick going, there will be no sentimental sacrifices on the part of the parents. It, too, will perish for it is the adults' job to stay alive, if possible, to breed again.

The three largest chicks were obviously doing very well. As soon as they realised there was no food, they began a desultory preening, poking and picking at the remaining down on their breasts. The two smaller ones fell asleep. Then the big ones started stalking around on the edge of the nest, stumbling clumsily over the heather stalks, dancing precariously on the sticks and flapping their wings energetically. It was only a matter of seconds before all three had involuntarily toppled out and, once recovered, were standing blinking with surprise. Then they began to show interest in exploring the surrounding heather. We hastily gathered them in, docile enough and not as yet alarmed by human beings, and placed them beside the rest of the family to pose for their photograph. While Don clicked away I put the finishing touches to the hide, bringing the tent with its supporting poles up to full height, and placing a camouflage net over the lot.

'Any sign of the adults?' Don asked as the two eldest chicks began making another determined effort to go adventuring.

I had been so absorbed with the youngsters that the almost routine behaviour of their parents had been forgotten. Don must have felt a tingling down his spine or something, for out of the blue, and silently, the two adult birds were winging towards us. Unswerving, unstoppable.

'Look out!' I hissed as, suddenly squawking loud protest, the harriers swooped straight for our faces.

We ducked, and they missed by inches, then banked away gracefully. With renewed shrieks of rage they came tearing in once more. Again and again, they flew in to harass us and each time we managed to evade the furious attack. I covered my eyes. The youngsters huddled together, sensing something wrong but not knowing what the fuss was all about.

'Right,' said Don, bending beneath yet another infuriated nose-dive and trying to gather together all his gear. 'This won't do. See me into the hide as quick as you can, then walk away. If they don't settle I'll signal and we'll leave them in peace.'

'Okay, but don't push them too far,' I cautioned, fearing that the hen was becoming so upset she might, even now, desert her young.

'Don't be silly. Of course I won't. Hurry up.'

I watched my husband's legs disappearing, with many a gasp and curse, beneath the heaving construction that was his hide and pushed in the tripod and rucksack after him. I smiled, thinking it was he who had to hurry, and wondering would the hide collapse about him before he was all set up. By now the hen harriers were circling high above our heads, not dive-bombing for the moment, but certainly not happy either.

'Okay,' came Don's muffled voice at last. 'Just check the outside, will you?'

I found a few large stones to anchor overhanging folds of cloth against further upheavals within and made sure that at least human eyes could not detect his presence there.

'You're all right,' I said. 'Good luck.'

He chuckled and gave me his final instruction.

'I'll signal when I want you.'

I tramped slowly away so that the adult hen harriers would see me leaving, and thanked heaven I had no pretensions to be, nor wish to become, a wildlife photographer. It is a stressful business. First and foremost there is concern for the subject that it suffers no harm as a result of your efforts; only long experience will tell you if you are pushing the creature too far. Then there is the care needed in setting up tripod and camera for the particular shot you want in as short a time as possible. Once ready, the tension involved is considerable: ears are pricked for every tiny sound;

through peepholes, eyes are straining for a warning glimpse of the creature's approach; fingers are poised, ready to release the shutter whenever that 'exact' moment of perfection is judged. Complete silence is necessary – no rustlings as you ease cramped limbs or make adjustments to the camera. It's all tough on the nervous system and is not for me.

The gorse thicket was where I was making for once more. It was far enough from the nest for the birds to lose interest in me and with the aid of a portable hide, which we always carried on these occasions, I should be more or less invisible. Both harriers circled round me as I walked and eventually they seemed to decide I did not represent danger to their family and veered away towards the new forest area to the east. I donned the hide, pushed my way in through the prickly bushes and sat on a boulder hoping I merged nicely with the scenery.

I need not have worried. In only a few minutes our hen came winging low over the moor and in her foot she carried a small bird. She swerved sharply away as she closed with the nest and flew to a perch on the branch of a willow not far away. Was the hide bothering her? Had she seen Don, his camera, or some unexpected movement that disturbed her? Or was it just a memory of human beings recently there? I waited on tenterhooks for the white handkerchief signal which might appear at any moment.

A temporary setback, only. Almost immediately, the bird rose from the branch, and circled once over my head. Then, prey still in foot, she flapped slowly back towards her nest. This time? Clamouring chicks may have helped. She glided over the top of the hide, altered course abruptly to approach her nest, then on wings spread broad and feet stretched long, dropped safely down. I imagined her youngsters crowding in to be fed and Don clicking merrily away. He told me afterwards that it had only been a meadow pipit that she brought and that did not go far amongst five hungry youngsters. The hen did not rise again, and I imagined her settling serenely over those of her brood who could still be accommodated beneath her body and wings, then closing her eyes. Taking the hint the rest of the family would collapse into the hollow of the nest and fall asleep too.

Almost an hour passed with nothing happening. The sun climbed high in the sky and was blazing down. It must be pretty uncomfortable in the hide, and on the nest bills would be agape as youngsters panted. The moor around me basked in the midday heat, the heather seeming to smoulder with hidden fires. On the horizon mirage-like images cheated me into all sorts of imaginings – human and animal presences, hillocks and lochs that were never there before, trees that had mysteriously grown. Behind me, the waters of the little lochan glinted in the sunshine, its small island shelter and shade to the family of mallards.

All at once a cry from above was no trick of the imagination. It was the sharp imperative of a harrier male calling to his mate: I have food for you, come and get it. I thought of Don in the hide, well aware of the lovely action that must follow and cursing that he would not be able to see it. He told me later that the hen's head had cocked sharply with the sound and at once she had risen clumsily from the nest, rustling the heather with the great flapping of her wings and rudely scattering the chicks. I watched her circle round twice, wings beating faster and faster to gain height, then soaring, straight as an arrow, up towards the cock. She looped elegantly over beneath him, a backwards somersault in slow motion, and neatly caught the prey that he released. Then she was sweeping back towards the earth and he, his duty done and now in no hurry, was flapping away to the plantation again. The hen levelled out some distance from the nest, winged slowly and ever-lower over the heather towards it, then dropped down beside her family.

It was at this moment that the peace of the morning was shattered and I immediately forgot the orderly happenings at a hen harrier nest. Men were shouting, dogs yapping excitedly, and the sound came echoing over the moor from somewhere behind me. With that ominous warning was a sudden stillness, and this tranquil place became hushed, vibrant with the helpless expectancy of its inhabitants. Men and dogs were there. What were they after?

The thoughts came tumbling. The Eagle Glen lay in that direction. Our wild vixen and her cubs were there. Had the hunters been at that den? Had an adult got away and they were after it, hoping to finish it off? Why could they not leave these animals alone? There were no sheep in the area, nor for miles around, no possible excuse or need to kill. I knew Don in his hide would be feeling angry and helpless, too, but there was nothing to be done by either of us. No laws were being broken. He told me afterwards he had decided it was best to stay put at least until something, or someone more distant than he, disturbed the hen and she flew from the nest; he did not want to frighten her by popping up close by. I think he also had romantic thoughts of defending the young chicks against rampaging terriers. For me, a more cowardly course. Not wanting to be accidentally shot, I threw off the camouflage cloak and stood on a rock in order to be seen.

I searched frantically ahead of the rabble and at last discovered their quarry, a rufous streak dodging in and out of the heather below the ridge to my right. A fox. It was limping badly, apparently from a wound in its left shoulder. Hell! They must have winged it, maybe at the den. Then another dismaying thought. Our presence could add to its problems. The breeze was only a gentle drifting in the air, but it was blowing directly from us towards the higher ground below which the animal was running. It must surely pick up our scent. And then, what? It would slow down while it tried to work out which way to go, and maybe give the dogs their chance. It surely hadn't a hope.

I watched the fox jinking through the heather, dipping in and out of ditches, keeping as low to the ground as its injury allowed. The terrain was rough and broken, dotted with large boulders, patches of heather and scree, and some ancient ditches dug long ago perhaps to drain the hillside. Not a great deal of cover, but maybe the animal knew of somewhere those dogs could not reach. I tried to make up my mind. Was it a dog fox or a vixen? Probably the dog; his mate was almost certainly shot at the den.

Then, for what seemed long moments, the fox disappeared and I dared to hope. Could it possibly have a safe place somewhere up there in a bank or a ditch? The pack came tearing through the heather, a motley collection, terriers scurrying this way and that trying to find a way through its entangling branches, collie dogs leaping, long and graceful, over obstacles as they appeared, and one eager springer spaniel, nose to the ground, racing ahead of them all. An untidy, unruly lot, hot on the scent of a fox, they bounded over the rocks, steeple-chased over the ditches, slithered through boggy patches still muddy in spite of the drought, all yapping their heads off with excitement in the fever of the hunt. Three men were toiling along some way behind.

The fox suddenly appeared on the bank of a ditch which ended just beneath the ridge. Not gone to ground, after all. A complete change of direction, though. Had it caught my scent? Perhaps. It stood poised, nose in air, ears pricked and eyes searching desperately for means of escape. And this was my first fleeting glimpse of the whole of the animal – no dog fox this, but a dainty vixen. Maybe the mother of the cubs in the Eagle Glen! The ground rose steeply beyond her to a cliff with smooth rockfaces and narrow ledges – useless to a fleeing animal with shot in her shoulder. But not too far off huge rocks, which at one time must have been a part of the heights above, might well have caverns beneath into which she could bolt. Perhaps that was the way she would go.

The pause to check was the vixen's undoing. She made for the gully and was easy to see as she moved in and out of the heather. The men, yelling encouragement, came running to catch up with the dogs. The dogs tumbled helter skelter into the ditch farther down its length, the quickest and shortest route. Hot on the scent of the fox, they tore along its bottom regardless of boulders, bog and vegetation. The men ran along the bank.

The vixen was tiring badly, limping worse than ever. Saliva dripped from her tongue, sullying the fur on her chest. At the top end of another ditch, she came to a stumbling halt, glanced briefly round at her tormentors, then disappeared again. What was she up to? Had she decided the gully was too far? Was she making for a hole somewhere beneath the cliff? Had she another safe haven she might reach? I felt time, and luck, were running out and willed her, in spite of her injury, to go for the cliff. That seemed the best bet.

The dogs came scrambling out of the ditch at its top, immediately picked up the scent again and were charging off along the cliff edge. Suddenly, all of them came skidding to a halt. In a patch of heather they stood uncertain, sniffing the vegetation, testing the air. Surely they couldn't have lost it again? Where was the vixen, for goodness sake? Could she possibly be safe? Then I remembered that it wasn't a ditch line they had stopped beside but a break in the heather which marked the course of one of the burns that flowed down the hillside to my right. It ended in the little loch.

The springer spaniel found the scent first and leapt over the bank, followed by the others all yelping with excitement. The vixen must be trying a last desperate stratagem to confuse her tormentors – a forlorn hope for there would be little water in the burn after the recent drought to dilute her scent. In a few seconds I spotted her at its mouth. At the same moment, with a start, I realised Don was standing quite still just behind me. There had been no sound of his coming. Unashamedly, I accepted an arm around my shoulders. In silence we watched our fox dragging through a bed of reeds, staggering through the bog which reluctantly released her dainty feet, and sinking at last into the water. She swam gamely for the little island, and perhaps the cool water was blessed relief to her overstretched body. The dogs made heavy weather of the soft ground, too, perhaps giving her a few minutes grace. Once in the water, though, they were gaining fast. It was quickly over. The vixen paddled bravely ashore, staggered lamely over its pebbles, then collapsed beneath their thrusting bodies and snapping jaws.

'Bloody hell!' I swore, and turned away.

'It's all over now,' said Don gently a few minutes later. 'The buggers!' And he did not mean the dogs. 'Come on,' he added. 'We'd better check on the hen. I think she was scared by all the noise. I've no idea which way she flew but I crawled out of the hide once she was away and hoped she didn't see me. She should be all right.'

It was good to have a diversion. The bird was alive, the fox dead. We must see her safely back on her nest. It was unlikely she would desert at this stage, chicks hatched and clamouring for food most of the time, but she had had a fright. We retreated to the gorse bushes and shared the portable hide after a fashion, knowing it might be just minutes or maybe the rest of the day before there was action. If she had, after all, deserted there would be nothing for it but to collect up the youngsters, take them home, and try to rear them ourselves.

'I'm almost sure that was the vixen from our den,' I said as we trained binoculars on to the harrier nesting area. 'The cubs are too young to manage on their own.'

'You can't be sure it was her,' comforted Don. 'Let's go up

tomorrow. It would be nice to see how the eaglets are getting on anyway.'

At that moment the harrier hen came flying steadily over the heather from the direction of the plantation. She held what looked like a grouse chick in her foot. Without hesitation she glided straight over the top of the hide and dropped down into her nest. Good. We could leave.

By this time the men had rounded up all their dogs and were walking away. They could not have failed to see us but, knowing our views, had avoided a meeting. The argument might have got out of hand and we lived in a small community. After a last look at the pebble beach where the torn remains of a vixen, her brush cut off, lay abandoned, we started the long trek home.

When at last we came to the old pine wood, late sunshine dappled the needle-covered floor, making it an enchanting place, and a rising wind creaked ancient branches into protest above our heads. A wren chattered in a nearby patch of heather. Something of the peace of long ago lingered there to calm my angry spirit.

An hour and a half later we were thinking that the riotous welcome from Shuna and Shian was even more exuberant than usual. They hate being shut away in the house when they know we are going for a tramp but have accepted that now and again it must be. This excitement at our return was not quite as usual. What had upset them? Once free, they raced across the garden and disappeared in the direction of the fox run. Hurrying behind them, we soon found out. Someone had cut a neat, fox-sized hole in the wire on the gate. Quite obviously it was deliberate, and a certain escape route for two small cubs which would have raced to see who was there. The dogs had known something was amiss, and Rufus and Rusty were almost certainly out and away.

Don swore, and my fertile imagination immediately conjured up all the awful things that could happen to two escaping fox cubs.

'First thing,' said Don, 'is to discover if they really have gone.'

'They're probably hungry,' I suggested. 'Why don't I fetch some food to tempt them with while you and the dogs make sure. Better check the fence for any other holes. Who do you think round here would do a thing like this? Those poor cubs are probably scared to death.'

'They won't be too far away,' replied Don cheerfully. 'They're too young to wander. Hurry up and get some rabbit pieces.'

I tend to panic on these occasions and, inevitably, they occur from time to time. Captive animals, especially foxes, do for one reason or another get out. You feel a terrible responsibility for creatures who, in spite of your best intentions, have learned to trust human beings and have become dependent on them. They have many enemies and usually you dare not advertise the escape in case the wrong people hear of it. There is little to be done other than to bait a live-catcher cage and hope hunger tempts them in.

Don was right this time, but not quite in the way he expected. I was just opening the fridge door to get out the rabbit when the phone rang.

'Your cubs are wrecking my kitchen!' wailed our neighbour of half a mile away. 'I'm sure they've broken all my precious china. You should hear the noise.'

My first reaction was delight. They were safe. My second: Oh god, poor Morag! I knew she collected old china and proudly displayed it on a lovely, antique kitchen dresser.

'We'll be right with you,' I reassured her, and dashed off to collect Don. Two would be required for this job.

He shook his head as I arrived.

'I'm pretty sure they're not in the den and the dogs have been all over the run. They're probably up a tree somewhere in the wood.'

'They're playing hide-and-seek in Morag's kitchen and she's not amused,' I retorted. 'Come on.'

We shut the dogs in the house and raced for the car.

'I don't know what they're up to but it sounds awful,' exclaimed Morag as we arrived at her garden gate.

The poor woman looked distraught and I could well understand. Foxes are extremely destructive creatures. Nothing in her room would be safe unless it was locked away in a cupboard or was completely out of reach. They would jump all over everything, hide beneath anything that could be squeezed under, try and scrape holes in carpets or rugs, and even climb the curtains. Add to this the panic of two terrified youngsters not knowing where on earth they had got to, and there would be problems.

'Right,' said Don, taking command at once. 'We'll try and catch them in the kitchen, but in case they give us the slip, Morag, shut all the passage doors.'

We could hear the rampaging youngsters long before we slipped quickly into the room, and one thing was immediately quite certain – they were not in the slightest bit upset or frightened. Bright appraising eyes glanced quickly our way. Instant recognition followed. But instead of rushing to greet us they set off once more to show us what a terrific time they were having. Perhaps in their minds one kitchen was much like another and they remembered their brief sojourn in ours. They were quite at home. Off they went again, Rufus leading and Rusty scampering after.

'Come on,' said Don, impatiently, as I stood aghast at the scene. 'Let's catch the little brutes.'

Both cubs were excited and not minded to be caught. After abortive attempts to grab we tried another tactic – sitting on the floor in the middle of all the chaos and trusting to curiosity, or greed for titbits, to bring them to us. It worked. Almost at once Rusty came trotting to my proffered hand and Rufus scrambled up Don's trousers and on to his lap. We popped the cubs quickly into their box with a couple of dog biscuits and tied the lid firmly down. Then we took a look at the damage.

They had been over the top of the Rayburn and, no doubt surprised by the heat from its covered hot plates, had knocked saucepans and a kettle to the floor. A rich vegetable soup was moving sluggishly over the lino, helped along by a faster-flowing rivulet of water. The deal table had long scratches on its scrubbed surface. The kitchen chairs had been knocked over. Two rugs were rumpled into peaks, valleys and tunnels. A scat had been dropped by the fridge and another by the washing machine. Pennies had been plentifully spent and the distinctive odour of fox was overpowering. One blessing. They had been on the dresser but by a miracle the precious china on its shelves had not been disturbed.

'I'll take them home and come back to give a hand,' said Don.

By the time he returned, we had done most of the work. He was laughing.

'They were not in the least put out by their adventure,' he said. 'Shrieks of joy when I put them back in the run. I've mended the gate and given them some rabbit. The dogs are on guard.'

'One of them actually had a pee in the sink,' our friend laughed. 'Wasn't that clever? Don't worry. The damage wasn't as bad as it looked. One broken coffee pot and a few scratches on the table which can be sanded. You two get home. I'll finish off.'

She was right. It was surprising how little real harm had been done. With windows and doors wide open, even the scent of fox was fading. We promised her a new coffee pot as soon as possible and Don would get to work on the table.

The fox in captivity is nearly always trouble for it is an accomplished escapologist. Its presence cannot be hidden – especially in country areas where your business is known far and wide. Both it and you will be regarded with suspicion and disapproval, for all foxes are a menace and should be destroyed before they get at the lambs, the local chickens, the domestic pets, or whatever. Usually safe enough while still appealing young cubs, once adult there is little hope for any who have escaped. Another less common threat is the person who considers it immoral to keep any wild creature in captivity, quite forgetting that it may be so for a perfectly sound reason, and forgetting too that it has become ill-equipped to survive in the wild. They cut a hole in the containing fence and think they have done the animal a good turn.

Rufus and Rusty were probably let out for a lark by village kids. This time, luckily, there had not been a tragedy.

FOUR

Wild Cat Island

'LET'S HAVE a spell,' I implored, hot, sticky and cross as we slogged up the last few yards to the top of the ridge.

'Okay,' teased Don. 'Don't you want to see the fox cubs?'

Afraid that the vixen who had been killed the day before was the mother of those we had watched, we were both anxious to find out what was going on at the den in the Glen of the Eagles and had, as planned, set out to visit it. There had been a problem though. The light breeze, now from the south, meant that the usual approach up the glen was impossible: our scent would have gone ahead of us and there would certainly have been no foxes to see. Instead, it had been a much longer walk. We had plodded over the wide expanse of the harrier moor, where the only easier walking was when we could follow deer tracks. We had laboured straight across the new plantation, in and out of endless furrows, until we came to a convenient ride which led in the right direction. Finally, we had scrambled to the top of the ridge through heather and boulders on a long steep slope. I, for one, needed a rest.

We found ourselves a perfect armchair situation, a hollow in the heather with large boulders dotted around. Two were good to sit against. Now we could admire the surrounding spectacular. The ridge stretched away to the south and on it, about half a mile away, was a cairn. It stood lonely and proud in a sea of heather and marked the point from which, in a little while, we would begin the stealthy stalk to the corrie of the foxes. To the north and west distant mountains, faraway giants reaching for the heavens, were fading into early evening mist. Beneath us the long narrow Glen of Tara stretched endlessly towards them. Sombre cliffs near its top rose in rugged steps to the far ridge, each ledge decorated in grass, heather and an occasional stunted rowan. A small wood of birches, on the hillside below, fluttered filigree leaves in the soft breeze. In the shadow of those towering heights, the little lochan, like a dark opal, was a matchless jewel in a wild and lonely setting. Wavelets now scurried to caress its rocky shores and, as always for me, it was a place where something exciting must surely happen and was therefore the focus of attention.

A small island floated greenly in the centre of the loch and safe from the maws of sheep was clad in willow scrub and birch. An old pine tree grew proud and crooked from out of a large patch of heather in the middle, battered and bent by all the winds of heaven, a monument to a more wooded era. Tall reeds fringed the rocky southern shore and shuddered gently in the breeze. A black-throated diver was fishing nearby and we wondered if her chicks, discovered bobbing along behind her a week or two back, were already among them snug asleep, small heads turned and laid over their backs. Fifty or more black-headed gull youngsters floated serenely on the brooding waters. Their parents were wheeling above in the clear evening sky, a noisy halo of perpetual movement declaring the day at an end. A small pebble beach marked the northern shore and it, too, was bordered in reeds.

We crouched in our resting place and were reluctant to move on. It was a glorious evening and there was plenty to see. A family of ravens, high above our heads, chattered amiably together as they flew towards the cliffs. They had done well this year, with five chicks fledged. From far beyond them, in a higher distance, we spotted a solitary eagle on widespread wings coasting in towards the Eagle Glen – presumably all was well with the eagle family. A short-eared owl, holding a vole in its foot, flapped slowly overhead towards the moorland beyond – maybe the one we had seen there before.

Suddenly a buck barked a warning from somewhere below in Glen Tara. The sound was distinctively roe deer, not to be confused with any other, and seemed to come from the birch wood on the far side of the lochan. It was unlikely the animal could have got our scent, so what was bothering it? Then we noticed the lower branches on one of the trees bending and

Golden eagle hen

Eagle feathers in
a misty Eagle Glen

Hen harrier cock joins his mate at the nest

Our hen harrier family in harmony

The first eaglet is born, a second egg is cracked

Fox cubs are sometimes prey for eaglets

The wild cat
prowls delicately
over the screes

Wild cat kitten

Angry defence

swaying backwards and forwards as if in a miniature whirlwind. A tawny shape was there, half seen, almost hidden by some tall bracken and the stem of the tree. All at once, it revealed itself, a roe buck butting his way through, the branches rudely pushed aside, then snapping back into sudden stillness. He stood on the open hillside, birches for background, rust-red coat glowing in the evening sunshine, a perfect picture of a dominant male animal surveying his domain. It was the time of the roe deer rut. Deceptively delicate of build, he seemed fighting fit and ready for any challenge. Restless, too. He began pawing the ground furiously, stamping impatiently, tossing his head and generally showing us what a fine fellow he was. Heather stalks flew everywhere, grass and soil erupted from beneath his impatient feet and though his six-point antlers were by this time clear of velvet, he kept turning to rub them vigorously up and down the branch that had first signalled his presence to us. Many of the nearby trees would already thus have been marked with his scent and, if necessary, he would fiercely defend his territory and guard the does within it.

Don nudged my arm.

'Can't you see him?' I exclaimed, thinking he had failed to spot the animal.

But Don was not watching roe deer at all. He was flat on his stomach and creeping closer to the edge of our hollow.

'Cat!' he breathed. 'Be quiet.'

Something much nearer than the buck, but farther down the hillside, had his complete attention. A wild cat? We should be so lucky! For several agonising moments I searched patches of rock, heather and bracken for a precious something which was sure to vanish from the scene before ever I caught a glimpse of it. At last, I had it and the adrenalin began to pump. There, among some boulders on a long scree slope, leafy fern hiding the greater part of the body, there was certainly a cat. In a shaft of evening sunlight, slit green eyes were glinting as they checked the rough hillside above and a short tail with dark, bulbous tip was twitching slowly. That tail could only belong to a true wild cat!

I had hardly taken in our good luck when the animal rose unhurriedly to its feet, stretched, yawned, then crawled forward a foot or two. Longer of body than the average domestic cat and standing taller, it stepped daintily on to a smooth-topped rock, curled itself round and round as if about to sink into sleep, but instead sat up again and began a thorough cleaning-up. Now was a wonderful opportunity to see the creature in all its glory and to confirm that it was indeed wild – no 'blotches' to spoil the regular narrow banding on its brindled fawn-grey sides and its tail perfectly marked with broad dark bands. The deep pink tongue worked busily as with voluptuous ease, the long neck stretching, it fastidiously covered the soft silky fur over shoulders, back, and dark dorsal stripe. Powerful haunches spread-eagled then, to allow a meticulous licking of the paler fur of chest, stomach and thighs. Now we could properly see the face – the beautiful fierce eyes, black-tipped nose, smallish ears, narrow stripes on the forehead, and a white muzzle with whiskers long and luxuriant.

'What a beauty!' I could not help whispering.

'Wonder what it's doing hanging about like this?' Don demanded.

'Not hungry and perhaps just enjoying the evening!' I suggested, with anthromorphological understanding.

'Oh yeah?'

It was a moment to set the heart beating faster and nothing on earth could have moved us from that hillside. Much-persecuted and therefore shy, wild cats are rarely seen. This one looked a good specimen, the genuine article and not one of the feral beasts, usually the progeny of wanderers from farms or country houses that have mated with their wild brethren. In spite of its status as a protected species, so often the wild cat seen is the one that has been shot, or is the victim caught in a snare which has not been checked regularly and often by a careless gamekeeper or shepherd.

In due course our cat seemed pleased with its toilet. It rose to its feet, stretched long rippling muscles in the glowing light of approaching sunset, then yawned a long yawn. We thought that, at last, it would sleep, but instead it looked carefully all about, then reached a paw downwards from the stone and began to pat a small object. It prodded playfully this way and that, apparently teasing something recently caught and still alive though crippled – surely a classic cat-and-mouse game and any moment the creature would be tossed into the air. Not a bit of it. In a few seconds our cat's head came abruptly up and the creature being roughly shaken into place in its mouth was not a mouse but a kitten. This cat was a female and, miraculously, blissfully, she had a family. There would surely be other kits. We quickly scanned the nearby ground but if they existed at all the kittens were well hidden in the heather.

The mother did not give us time to search for long. Suddenly she shook her youngster into a safer hold, teeth white against the softest and darkest of fur and the tiny head a perfect replica of her own, then straight away started off down the hillside. What was she up to? Where was she going? Tingling nerves told me this was something special, but how could we not lose a small, perfectly camouflaged creature on a hillside that gave her plenty of cover?

'Shall we try to follow her?' I asked, afraid we would lose her almost at once.

'Better to stay put,' Don replied. 'We wouldn't have a hope. Keep your eyes glued.'

The cat flitted surprisingly quickly downhill, all grace and fluid movement, threading first a sure-footed way through the rubble and boulders of the scree without a single pebble sent carelessly scurrying away. She streaked over that treacherous slope, neatly, delicately, as though it were made of velvet and nice soft going. Crouching low to the ground, muscles rippling beneath her gleaming coat, blunt, broad-ringed tail curving down to its tip and bending from side to side with the movement of her body, she fled over the rough terrain. In jaws that could kill mountain hare or roe deer fawn, the tiny swinging tail-and-head-hanging-down bundle was firmly held by the scruff. Once off the scree, she slowed a little, padding steadily on, concealing her flight in the heather and peeping round each large boulder to check before proceeding onwards. Her air was purposeful, as if she very well knew what she was about. Which, of course, she did.

Then the inevitable happened. Suddenly, she had vanished. One moment a fascinating living creature doing something interesting, the next she might never have been there at all.

'Can you see her?' Don asked anxiously.

'No,' I replied. 'I've lost her in that patch of heather above the burn. She'll surely show up again in a minute?'

'Hope so. Try to keep an eye on the shore and any clear

ground. I'll stay fixed on the spot where we last saw her.'

The burn, now only a trickle after the rare summer drought, had in times of flood worn a deep rocky bed through the heather, forging over long years a small, narrow gully. Nearer the lochan, on a more gradual gradient, it meandered first through a patch of bog myrtle and then through a bed of reeds. One minute our cat was prowling through the heather on the top of the nearer bank of the burn, next she had apparently gone to ground in one or other of these excellent hiding places. For all we knew she was crawling up the hillside again or had a den somewhere in that gully. We could only wait and see, but as the minutes passed with no sign of that streamlined creature, so beautifully designed to merge with the landscape, we became anxious.

Beyond the reeds was a small beach where the burn trickled into the loch. It was sandy and dotted with small stones. Washed by perpetual waters, the sand was pristine clean and the stones crystal polished in the rays of the evening sun. The last place to look for a cautious, secretive creature you would think, but on a routine check at a lucky moment I had her.

'She's right beside the loch. On the beach!' I nearly shouted, the relief was so great.

The gulls would soon have given the game away, anyway. As the sinuous body of our wild cat crept over the beach, kitten still safely on board, they rose in a cloud from the water and became a seething confusion of grey, white and black, wheeling and whirling overhead: this is our place, get out. Then they came tumbling down from the sky to flutter right over the animal. Rising and falling on restless wings, they hovered just above her screaming angry objection to her presence.

The cat, perhaps driven mad by the clamour of the angry birds, at last dropped her kitten and with a paw holding it safe, whiskers bristling and ears flattened, turned to swear at each attacker as it came. With teeth bared, eyes flashing, and no doubt growling too, she glared fierce defiance: this is my child, leave me alone. And, after a while, the gulls, perhaps realising there was nothing to be gained from bullying this creature, or bored, gave up. They began to peel away in ones and twos, to land with clumsily braking wings and feet in the loch below. In due course all were bobbing placidly beside their young.

Puss recognised her moment. She took her infant into her

mouth and began stalking towards the water. Not too easily seen, once in amongst the pale gleaming greys, browns and ivories of the small pebbles, perfect camouflage for that long slim body, we watched her come to a halt just where the ripples from the loch gently stroked the shore. And . . . with never a pause to look at the gulls, she marched straight into the water!

'Cats don't like water,' I gasped.

'This one evidently does,' Don chortled. 'Interesting.'

The wild cat breasted in as if this was a perfectly normal and oft undertaken course of action. There was no hesitation and she seemed to know exactly what she was about. Straight away swimming, she made steadily towards the little island. Bedraggled kitten limp in her mouth, but safe, she took no notice at all when the gulls renewed their frenzied attentions. She rose confidently from the dark waters when she arrived at the far shore and dropped her youngster at her feet while she shook out her coat. She gave the gulls, now returning to the water, a long appraising look then, sleek and shining, moisture still dripping from her underparts, lifted the kitten into her mouth and ran for the nearby reeds.

'She's made that journey before,' I remarked, full of admiration and amazement, but noting the casual air with which it had all been done.

'Looks like it. She certainly knows what she is doing,' Don agreed.

'Could she possibly have a den on the island?'

'Seems an unlikely place. How would she keep her family in food?'

The cat, meantime, had vanished. She had crawled into a small tunnel in the reeds and not reappeared. I did not panic, for the island was so small we could hardly mislay her for long. She probably had a coorie place where she could rest, right in the centre of the patch. While Don kept his eyes on the reeds, I took a quick look at the island.

The small beach where the cat had landed was on the side closest to our hillside, the reeds at its edge the place where she had disappeared. The far shore was protected by rocks awash with wavelets, and another bed of reeds with much thicker vegetation, mostly willow scrub. We reckoned the black-throated diver must have nested somewhere on their edge, right beside the water. In the centre of the island and surrounded by heather, the ancient pine stood proud guardian of a wild place untouched by the hand of man. Once upon a time there must have been two pines for an old stump stood forlorn and crumbling beside it, spread-eagled roots laid bare by eroding soil, the rest of the rotting stem fallen and crumbling into the heather.

A flicker of movement turned out to be the mother cat. She had worked through the reeds and now was crouching on the edge of the heather patch, apparently checking the way ahead. And it seemed there were no problems. In a second, she was flying over it, a tawny streak, kitten safely held, bounding over each bushy plant as an athlete might glide over a hurdle. She stopped dead once more beside the straggling roots of the old pine stump. Now the surprise. Our cat leapt lightly from one to the other of them, sure-footed, with never a stumble or pause to look back, and then started up the lichen-covered trunk. Forepaws stretched to reach high, sharp claws digging in, hindlegs springing to match, dark-barred tail streaming away behind, she scrambled quickly up and achieved the jagged top at last. For a second she stood poised, green eyes flashing for us in the evening sun, then turned away. With forepaws reaching down for safe hold, she slithered out of sight. That stump was hollow!

'Well I'm damned!' exclaimed Don.

'I'll bet you've never seen a wild cat do that before,' I said, amazed.

'No way. I'm sure we're right, though. She's made that journey before and knows exactly what she's doing.'

Wild cat mothers often move their families from one den to another, perhaps for reasons of security or maybe because the one in use has become soiled. It seemed incredible, however, that in order to do so, one would confidently enter water and swim quite a distance with a kitten in her mouth, and that the little creature had not drowned in the process.

Two minutes later, perhaps long enough to give her kit a quick licking, our cat came creeping from that strange place for a den. First a cautious head was seen, then the whole of her lithe body briefly poised on the stump's serrated edge. There was no kitten in her mouth. She sprang lightly down to the ground and began to retrace her steps. Once again she made her way through the reeds, once more she scurried across the shore and entered the water, yet again the gulls protested. She paddled confidently on and, in due course, rose smoothly on to the other shore and made straight for the reeds. In seconds she was on the bank of the burn and then climbing the hillside towards the spot where we had first seen her. We sat spellbound, foxes and time completely forgotten.

The cat was obviously in a hurry, anxious perhaps to collect all of her family together. Unencumbered now, she bounded lightly from boulder to boulder, worked her way with few diversions to left or right up the slippery scree and finally jumped on to the rock where we had first seen her cleaning up her coat. There she paused a moment to look carefully around, then padded softly, secretly, towards a massive boulder with blaeberry growing on the top. It was only a few yards away and perfectly visible from our watching place. We should have spotted the small cavity beneath it long ago. Our cat crept down into its shelter.

'That must be where her kittens were born!' I exclaimed.

'Hush,' Don whispered. 'She might hear you.'

When a few minutes later she emerged, we were not surprised to find another youngster, small, striped and helpless, in her mouth. Down the hill she set off, the same route as before, over the steep scree, into the gully and on through the bog myrtle and into the reeds. With the same slinking sureness of purpose we expected her at any moment to be crossing the little shore to the loch. Not this time. Suddenly, for no reason that we could see, she was crouching low, almost melting into the reeds nearby, only her head visible and the kitten in a crumpled heap at her feet. She was quite motionless and had we not known she was there I doubt if we would have discovered her.

We did not speak, both sensing that only something threatening would bother her. But what was it? All at once, from somewhere behind us, an enormous dark bird came winging over the glen, the sinking sun enhancing the golden glow of its feathering, the head down with sharp eyes searching. An eagle! No wonder the cat was still. This was a bird who would kill a wild cat if the opportunity arose and this one, almost certainly, had a hungry family to feed in the Eagle Glen. Our cat surely had problems – her own survival, a kitten, and a family waiting for her in her new den.

The eagle came gliding downwards, not a threat as yet but perhaps curious. Then it was fluttering, wings flapping hard, right above the cat. The animal, at bay, glanced briefly up and knew she must move. Reeds were useless cover against this great bird. She picked up the kitten, dashed straight out of the reedbed and began running over the shore towards the loch. The eagle came hurtling down. The cat dodged sideways, then leapt for the rippling waves. She plunged in with a tremendous splash, water cascading white and sparkling skywards. The eagle, taken by surprise, veered sharply away seconds before contact. Without audible protest it climbed steeply, effortlessly, for the sky.

By now, of course, we had a commotion of gulls all squawking angrily as they rose from the lochan. They began swirling round and round overhead, warning their youngsters of danger with raucous shrieks and squawks. The eagle took stock, floating lazily on the evening air, sizing up the possibilities, ever watchful but in no great hurry. The cat paddled on for dear life, breasting the water aside, kicking hard, ploughing a course towards her island. No time was wasted trying to see what her enemy was up to, though she must have been conscious of that menacing presence above. The kit was still in her mouth.

'That's a hen eagle,' Don said quietly. 'It's probably from the Eagle Glen.'

'Could be,' I replied. 'I wonder if that kitten will drown.'

The gulls were useful to the cat. The eagle, for all its size, probably did not like their fearful clamour and would be hesitant of plunging through their swarming mass. As well, there was water beneath them, an unaccustomed element in which it would not even attempt to catch prey. Instead it played safe, gliding round and round over the little loch, patiently awaiting the moment when it could attack again. For a short while the cat was left in peace, and as she neared the island, still doggedly swimming, the gulls lost interest too, peeling away in ones and twos and gradually coming to rest beside their young.

As the fleeing mother came floating in towards the shore, kitten limp and dripping in her mouth, the eagle began sinking again, lower and lower and eerily silent. In a few seconds it was hovering over its victim once more, head down and talons flexed.

'Can she possibly make it?' I whispered, thinking, of course, of the cat.

'Who knows?' was the best Don could manage.

The cat rose out of the water, a small tidal wave of flurrying droplets. Without a pause to shake herself she started off across the shore. The eagle came scissoring down. Cat, spitting hate, leapt neatly aside. Eagle, swift and deadly in attack but clumsy in recovery, swerved awkwardly away, banked right, then swept with careless ease into the sky. Cat dashed for the reeds and her tunnel. A dark menacing shape, seemingly disdainful, fluttered endlessly overhead.

'Surely it will give up now?' I agonised, my maternal feelings for the kitten family getting the better of me.

'It's got youngsters to feed, too.'

The cat kept moving, low to the ground, kitten still safe but looking pretty lifeless. She jinked over the pebble shore, then suddenly seemed to know there was no time to reach the bed of reeds. The majestic bird came swooping in. She swung round on a fivepenny piece, abruptly changed course, and began racing towards a large rock not far away. It must have been an old friend in need. She slipped into the hollow beneath it, as one reaching a known safe haven, just as the eagle stalled and reached wicked talons to grab. As she turned to face her enemy, there may have been a brief meeting of eyes, sizing-up and hating. There was certainly another spitting, snarling message from the cat: you can't get me here. Once more the tireless bird had been thwarted.

You would have thought that was it. The predator knew exactly where its prey was hiding, would know that it would not move from its shelter, would surely, at last, recognise defeat. Now was the moment to give up. Something, however, made that huge, dignified creature, all ruffled feathers and fierce dark eyes, behave in a most undignified manner. Still hovering above the big boulder, it began to sink towards the rock once more, feet stretched out as if for a landing. Finally, touch-down was accomplished with meticulous good judgment and never a wobble. At once, with head poked inquisitively forward, curiosity not greed apparently the motivation, it began stalking for the edge. The cat cowered lower to the ground. The kitten lay unmoving. The bird took one more pace forward . . . and, totally concerned with finding its quarry, stepped into space! There was a flurry of frantic wings as it righted itself by a miracle, then, perhaps tired at last of a fruitless venture, it rose above the little lochan and flapped off in the direction of the Eagle Glen.

This had been nature truly at work. A formidable predatory bird had hunted an equally formidable mammal with a youngster to protect and had not been successful. It had been both interesting and astonishing. Two humble human beings knew they were most unlikely ever to see this happen again.

There was no time to relax. The cat remained where she was only long enough to make sure her assailant had departed, then giving her kitten a perfunctory lick – a tiny front paw made small protest at a rough tongue rasping – she gathered it up, stalked quickly through the reeds to the heather and then raced for the pine stump.

'What luck we came this way!' I whispered, still up in the clouds and forgetting there was no particular need to be quiet.

'I wonder how many kittens there are?' was Don's more down to earth concern as he began wiping his face with anti-midge preparation. I had not even noticed the midges.

'And why was she moving her family?' I wondered.

'Could be any one of several reasons. Maybe a fox disturbed her at the other den, or even fox hunters.'

The sun would soon be setting. It was high time we were away to the fox den if we wanted to be able to see anything. Difficult to leave, though. As always on these occasions, there was the nagging feeling that, against the odds, there might be more action. The wild cat might appear again. But within the next few minutes she did not, and if she only had two kittens, the family was now complete. It seemed likely, too, that after her recent experience she would stay under cover at least until it was dark.

'Let's go,' said Don, rising stiffly to his feet and stretching.

'Do you think we could possibly get on to that island?' I asked, as we made our way quickly up the hillside towards the ridge.

'It would be great to get some photographs,' he agreed. 'But I don't think it would work. The island's too small and there's no real cover.'

'We must try and see that family again.'

'Probably this is as good a place as any. A good height above the lochan, little chance of being scented and a good view of the pine.'

'I'm greedy,' I laughed.

As we hurried along the ridge, harder work this time since we must keep below the skyline to avoid a silhouette picture reaching foxes in the Eagle Glen beyond, I imagined our cat comfortably in her safe place, the kittens nuzzling and kneading into her soft warm belly.

When we came to look down on it, most of the Eagle Glen was in shadow, the sun long vanished behind the ridge we had just traversed. The sombre cliffs of the eyrie were enshrouded in gloom, and though we could just see the giant pile of sticks through binoculars, it was more that we knew it was there and could imagine every detail. Imagination also conjured up two young eaglets settled for the night, solemnly standing with eyes closed at the back of a flattened nest. Their cat-bullying mother was probably beside them.

As on our previous visit, the fox den could be seen in the last of the evening light. We paused above it, ready to scramble down the steep slope into the corrie, and noted the breeze still gently blowing up the glen and into our faces. Excellent. A quick look round and, so far as we could tell, there were no foxes about. We dropped down from the top, slowly since it was difficult not to send stones bouncing ahead of us down the scree, and then edged into position on a convenient ledge.

It was as well we had been careful. Foxes were already about. Maybe they had only just emerged but three cubs were sitting at the entrance to the den, caught in the last of the sunshine, and looking as though they were unsure what to do next. Perhaps they were waking up after a long day's sleeping. In a minute or two, one by one, they found energy enough to rise to their feet, stretch their long lean bodies and yawn. One by one, they pottered over to pieces of hare lying scattered not far away, sniffing at them and picking them up to chew. One challenged another for possession but was snarled at for its pains. There must have been little meat on the bones anyway, for soon they were all sitting about aimlessly scratching and yawning once more. Three young foxes expecting a parent to bring them food. Two apparently missing. And no sign of the vixen.

Time passed. No adults arrived. The cubs became restless, popping in and out of the den and sitting about yawning, doing nothing. This could be perfectly normal. Perhaps both parents were long in finding prey, and the cubs, becoming more and more hungry, were growing increasingly restless. This was feasible, but I had an uneasy feeling that all was not well.

'Have you seen more than three?' whispered Don suddenly.

'Don't think so.'

'Hm. I wonder.'

'I suppose they're beginning to wander a little further now,' I suggested.

'Maybe. I think that's one of the males down there, and the two little females. The others must be bolder fellows and away hunting.'

I think we were both troubled by now, and the ever-increasing darkness did not help. The rough sides of the corrie seemed to shrink, creeping closer as the light faded, their giant boulders menacing and inspiring the thought that something was wrong. We sat on as long as there was light enough, even keeping our binoculars fixed on two separate and likely places once the surrounding terrain was featureless. The three youngsters eventually wandered off, disappearing into the surrounding vegetation, no doubt to hunt voles. Once we caught a small shape leaping and pouncing. The vixen did not come to check on her family, or bring food to them, and though earlier the cubs had been looking expectantly down the corrie to the hillside beyond, the dog did not materialise with prey. Our unrest was the memory of a vixen killed on the moor and the near certainty that she was the mother of this family.

'Well,' said Don, at last, as reluctantly we gave up. 'We don't know for sure that anything's wrong. The others will probably turn up.'

I hoped he was right. We crept on down the corrie to the burn below. The journey through the glen was slow, so dark that we had many a stop to check with torches that we were on the right track. Now and again, too, when a thought occurred, we paused to discuss the situation at the den. It did seem as though the vixen was missing and the cubs still too small to manage on their own. Our hope was that the dog would take care of them. It was difficult not to be concerned for the only surviving fox cub family in our area. We would come again, as soon as possible, to check on how they were doing.

When at last we arrived home, there occurred one of those strange examples of human contrariness that never cease to puzzle me. Peter, the gamekeeper from a nearby estate, was waiting outside our gate. He looked relieved to see us.

'You're late, Peter,' Don said as we emerged somewhat stiffly from the van. It was well past midnight. 'What brings you at this time of the evening?'

'I've something to show you.'

I guessed what was coming.

'It's a beauty,' he added, opening up the back of his vehicle.

It was indeed a beauty. A half-grown fox cub, a fine young male with lustrous, almost rufous-coloured eyes and a beautiful thick brush, was lying on the floor, tied to a heavy log. He sprang panting to his feet, alarmed by the presence of strangers, but relaxed when he saw Peter standing beside us. The tail began to wag and friendly fox-greeting noises filled the van. Obviously a very tame animal.

'What's wrong?' Don asked, knowing perfectly well.

'He's getting too much for my wife now he's growing bigger.'

There was a pause, no doubt while we were supposed to digest the implications of this statement.

'I'm away all day and can only see to him in the evening,' he continued. 'So he has to be shut in a shed all the time. I'm wondering whether you would take him?'

'Oh, Peter,' I said sorrowfully, well-acquainted with this oft-occurring sad plea. 'You know perfectly well we can't, much as we would love to.'

He looked innocent. 'I thought he could join your two.'

'Not a hope,' said Don firmly. 'Rufus is a male and there would be trouble later on.'

'Oh, well.' He laughed, ruefully. 'It was worth a try.'

'How did you do this year?' asked Don casually, referring to the annual visit to the fox dens.

'I think we got most of them,' Peter replied, 'but a few always get away. And that keeps me in a job,' he added, with a laugh.

Thus a strange, almost annual irony was re-enacted. The gamekeeper who back in April had visited a fox den, had shot both of the adults and sent in his terriers to destroy the cubs, then had been quite unable to kill the appealing little object which came crawling out a little later, probably looking for its siblings. Almost instinctively, Peter would have grabbed the tiny cub before the terriers could get at it, would have popped it gently into his warm pocket and then carried it safely home for his wife to love and look after. Now it had become a problem.

'Do you think', I asked Don as Peter drove away and my mind wandered back to the den in the Eagle Glen, 'that eagles take fox cubs for prey?'

'I'm sure they do,' he replied. 'And wild cat kittens too, if they are out of their den during the day.'

FIVE

Runaway Rufus

I PAID SEVERAL MORE late evening visits to the fox den in the Glen of the Eagles, anxious to find out what was going on there. Each time it looked more and more deserted. No bones, fur or feathers were scattered around. The much-padded paths through the heather no longer looked used and even the grass in front of the den was springing back to life. It seemed certain that there was no cub activity now. His mate missing, the dog could have led his family to another den, but there appeared to be no particular reason why he should – no evidence, for instance, of any disturbance by fox hunters. Perhaps he just had failed to bring them food, in which case there might be a dead body or two lying around. I could not find one and could only guess at what had happened.

I had been impatient, too, to go back to Glen Tara in the hope of another glimpse of the wild cat family. Don had felt it wiser to leave her alone for a while, arguing that it was most unlikely she would move her kits unless forced to do so by disturbance of some sort or a shortage of prey. The resources of that little island were strictly limited. It would be good to know how she was managing to keep them in food. At last, the moment seemed right. We would go. At the weekend, not with the greatest of expectations, we set off well before dawn.

The breeze was from the north so there was no long tramp over the moors to Glen Tara and we were able to use the shorter route through the Eagle Glen. But it was a slow picking of our way, in near darkness, up the familiar track alongside the burn, its waters tinkling merrily but the bird world not yet come to life.

We sensed creatures of the night slinking away as they discovered our passing. We paused for a moment beside the marker rock where the climb to the eagle eyrie commenced. Nothing could be seen of the nest, but the brooding presence of its guardian cliffs struck deep into the consciousness of two mortals passing by. In due course, we crawled on all fours up the final slope and crept into our 'armchair' viewpoint. A pale sky tinged with pink promised sunrise soon.

We looked down now on a changed world. Dusk had been the sun departing in a blaze of glory to the west, bathing the hillsides of the glen in a golden glow. Dawn was its rising over the eastern ridge of the Eagle Glen, the cliffs of the faraway eyrie now aflame. The hillside below us was shadowed, still untouched by its radiance, but the small lochan reflected light from the sky. The receding planes of sombre hillsides were pictured there, and a softly feathered covering, gently shifting and stirring, was the gullery not yet quite awake. The island was a place of mystery in the centre, its all-important pine stump a dark silhouette reflected in the quiet water. Beside it was another reflection. Its living companion, tall and proud, stood sentinel over a wild cat's den.

The light gradually improved, reflections faded, birds began a chorus to welcome the day, and a golden sun rose over the ridge behind. The little island with its rocky shores, its pebble beach and reed bed, and its heather clearing was miraculously transformed into a brilliant setting for whatever might come. Our eyes went straight to the place that mattered. And it was a place well-used. The rim at the top of the stump was minus some of its jagged teeth. Strips of lichen on the stem had been torn away. Narrow secret paths, not there before, threaded the heather. Scratch marks, surely from sharp kitten claws, decorated the old pine roots.

'Looks good,' whispered Don.

I nodded. 'No sign of our roe buck friend.'

'He'll have got everything sorted out. There should be a doe with a fawn by now. Keep an eye open.'

Half an hour later, there was still no sign of cat or kittens and I, for one, was becoming anxious. Had we missed her? Perhaps she had gone off to hunt before we arrived, had already returned with prey and was now curled up in the den with the kittens. Or perhaps she had taken them to another den.

'We'll give her an hour,' said Don, reading my thoughts.

That would certainly be the limit. By then the sun would be well up, the cat's island home brightly lit and there would be little chance she would emerge with too much light and no cover. We agreed that Don would watch the island and I the hillside below.

The raven family of our last visit had woken up and was cavorting in the cloudless sky above us. The five youngsters were taking part in a display of aerobatics to impress their parents who were flying more soberly side by side. Diving towards the earth, tumbling as if intent on suicide, swooping up again to roll over and over, they stretched their wings and exercised after a long night's roosting. Then, as if a command had been given, all were making towards the Eagle Glen ridge, 'speaking' to each other with gruff raven voices, parents steady on course, youngsters still tangling. They alighted, and all with poking, probing bills began strutting around to see what grubs might be won. No eagles, buzzards, harriers or short-eared owls were to be seen. No lone fox went slinking to cover after the short night's hunting. You can't have everything!

It was another half hour before we had any action. Suddenly I caught a tiny movement in the reeds where, on that other occasion, the wild cat had crouched before her dash to the lochan. A tall stiff stem sprang back into place, another leaned away from something prowling there. Surely that was a few inches of narrow, dark barring on a rabbit-fur coat? Our cat, at last.

'Do you see her?' I whispered, not turning to Don in case I lost her.

He chortled quietly. 'I see a kitten! On the top of the pine stump.'

'Hell! I daren't look. The mother is in the reeds.'

'Good. Don't lose her.'

Then, hiatus time again. Nothing more happened. The adult was surely there, still crouching in the reeds. It would be difficult to miss her if she made a move. Perhaps she was resting. Don told me the kitten was still sitting on the top of the stump, wobbling precariously while trying to clean its whiskers.

'Two now,' he suddenly exclaimed. 'There is one on the roots.

It must have been asleep. Now it's climbing the stem. The other one is boxing its face. Kitten games. Both look in good nick – she must be feeding them well.'

At this moment, to my great relief, for I was dying to take a look at the kits, the adult crawled cautiously out on to the pebbles. She was gripping a bird in her jaws, a limp bundle of rufous feathers which must be a grouse. Rather lanky and lean, I thought. You must be having a hard time keeping yourself and the kits in food. The cat took a quick look round, then crept straight for the water, dragging the bird as best she could. As she breasted in and headed straight for the gently floating flotilla, the gulls, perhaps well-used to this strange creature now, just paddled hurriedly aside to let her through. Early morning preening was resumed at once.

The cat would take a few minutes to reach the island. I risked a look at the pine stump. And gasped.

'Nice aren't they?' Don teased. 'I thought you'd like a surprise!'

Four, not two, small creatures were playing a rollicking kitten game among the roots at its foot. I thought back to that long arduous journey of the mother's, from hillside home to island, from shore to shore over quite a large expanse of water, and a battle with an eagle. Four separate trips. It was staggering.

'Mum's on the way with food,' I warned. 'She's in the water.'

'Great. This should be interesting.'

The kitten game was dainty, fierce, and above all quick. A jumping over, crawling under, leaping from one to another of the old pine roots. A rolling over on to backs, a boxing, biting, and a kicking. A sudden breaking away of one little creature into the heather, and the rest chasing after it to pounce and start the game all over again. Four beautiful kittens which, through the glasses, looked as if they were more or less faithful replicas of their elegant mother – dark striping on faces and bodies, each with a dark dorsal stripe, and thick rings barring shortish tails with the obligatory dark bulbous end. Each kit would be marked slightly differently but from the distance it looked as though we had four true wild cat kittens that might, with luck, survive to adulthood.

'She's just coming out of the water,' I reported.

'And they know it,' chuckled Don.

He was right. The great romp had come to an end. Four small statues were posed motionless on the old pine roots, heads turned towards the lochan. No way could they see their mother, as yet. How did they know she was coming? Instinct? Or could they have scented her? All at once, they were springing into life and scampering through the heather to meet her. We lost them in the reeds.

The adult came swimming in placidly. She rose out of the water, dropped the grouse, gave herself a quick shaking, looked quickly skywards as if remembering a predatory bird, then picked up her burden and made for the reeds. She disappeared, and for perhaps thirty seconds we saw neither cat nor kittens. Then a commotion started where the reeds met heather. Still gripping the bundle of rufous feathers, her family doing its best to relieve her of it, the mother cat came running for the stump and, with a final leap on to its roots, dropped the grouse for her family.

She sat quietly by, drying off her dripping coat and licking it into shape, while her kittens squabbled over their bloody meal. Feathers flew as they tore at it. Fur flew as they fought each other. No doubt much spitting and growling was going on as well. Four little spitfires all competed fiercely for a share. The adult made no attempt to take some for herself, and once again we wondered how much food she was getting. That thin body probably told a tale.

By now the day was bright. Time for kittens to be safely hidden from eagles, buzzards and any other predators that might be around. The wild cat mother rose to her feet, yawned, and maybe 'spoke' to her family. She leapt in among them, pulled what remained of the bird into her mouth, and then took a running jump at the stump. Momentum took her safely to the top and her greedy kits scrambled after her. She paused to check on her family (for us, one last glimpse of a truly superb creature, all sprung steel and unbelievably graceful), then dropped down out of sight into her den. One by one, the kittens followed.

And then there were none! Suddenly, the whole episode might never have happened. We sat savouring the experience and congratulating ourselves on our luck. Perhaps quite a few people have caught glimpses of a wild cat now and again, but not many will have watched one doing the things ours had done. What were the chances of seeing the family just one more time?

'We'll have to come again soon,' I said to Don after we had calmed down a bit.

'Yes. She's got a problem, hasn't she? Kittens getting bigger and hungrier. Prey to be caught. And each time, a trip over the ocean to bring it to them.'

'Not only that,' I added, smiling. 'They're too big now to be carried back to dry land.'

It was difficult to come down to earth but we had another plan for the weekend and wanted to be home by the end of the morning. We would return to Glen Tara as often as possible in the hope of catching the wild cat mother at the crucial moment when she would have to make a decision. If unlucky, we could at least look for clues. Now we set off along the ridge after a long last look at the magic stump.

The fox den was examined with binoculars from the top of the corrie as we passed. Though not expecting to see any action, for the cubs would long ago have hidden themselves away for the day, we were hoping for signs that they were, in spite of our fears, still about. But it all looked so completely unused, so utterly deserted, that it was difficult to believe a fox family had ever been there. We did not wait.

Very soon we were scanning the whole of the Eagle Glen. So far as we could tell, there were no eagles soaring high above and keeping an eye on us, and neither of them was standing on the eyrie or on a look-out point somewhere in the glen. From a distance, the old hide looked as solidly secure as ever, a permanent landmark they would long ago have become used to. We continued on, following the usual route from the fox den when approaching the eyrie from the ridge, and hoped to enter the hide unobserved. The sun was now high in the sky and the deer-path trail easy to follow.

'There's a nice lot of whitewash,' I commented with satisfaction as we came nearer and a waterfall of droppings could be seen decorating the cliff.

'I wonder how many there are,' Don added, knowing how unlikely it was that both chicks would have survived as long as this.

In a short while we were picking our way carefully down and keeping as close as possible to the cliff face. By now it was really warm and I wondered how much shelter from the sun the eaglets would have. The old ewe, which had been there on our last visit, was still tranquilly grazing as if she had never been away, and her lamb, now quite big, was frolicking with two others not far away. They ignored us. We clambered up the huge boulder to the hide as quickly as possible and crawled in through the small entrance at its rear. It was hot and dusty, and the dead bracken crackled as we settled down.

'Well, I'm damned!' exclaimed Don, already at a peephole.

'Only one eaglet?' I asked.

'There's good news for the farmer!' he chuckled quietly.

'What do you mean?'

'Take a look.'

Two healthy young eaglets stood solemnly on the sticks. Terrific. But that was not the point. At the back of the nest, where ledge met sheer cliff, lay two crumpled bundles of red fur. Two small brushes, both with a white tip, were still attached.

'Our missing fox cubs!' I exclaimed.

'Perhaps,' Don acknowledged, more cautious.

But the cubs were long dead, the chicks very much alive and we had come to check on their progress. We would talk about this later. So, two eaglets. By now the smaller would be out of danger from its sibling though we noted a wound still healing on its head. Both were staring at the hide as if our arrival had been observed, but neither seemed bothered. They looked remarkably well-fed, as the indescribably messy state of the eyrie would suggest. Skins, bones and uneaten flesh lay everywhere and a malevolent cloud of buzzing bluebottles rose and fell in angry competition around them. Eaglet waistcoats were nicely speckled and the feathering on wings and backs was dark – standing facing us, as they were, we could not see the white that would be on wings and tail. Not too far from fledging, we reckoned.

'I'd like to take a look at that wound,' Don remarked. 'Check on that drooping wing, too. The bird may not be able to fly.'

'Better not wait too long,' I suggested. 'They'll soon be ready to go. Aren't they beautiful?'

Neither of the adults arrived at the eyrie while we were there and, of course, we did not really expect them. Now the young were so large and prey evidently plentiful, the parents would be coming in only occasionally. In a few more minutes we left the hide as unobtrusively as possible and started for home.

'Have you ever seen fox cubs on an eagle eyrie before?' I asked Don, as we tramped down the hillside towards the burn.

He had far more experience of eagles than I did.

'Several times. It's idiotic, really. Farmers and shepherds spend a lot of time and money trying to wipe out the fox, and often the eagle too, if they think they can get away with it. Yet in these parts eagles, if left alone, would probably control fox numbers perfectly adequately.'

This was one of Don's favourite hobby horses, and we could have had quite a discussion on our way down the burn towards the bottom of the glen. But we had planned a great adventure for Rufus and Rusty and there was need to hurry.

Our two cubs were now about ten or eleven weeks old and growing into proper little foxes. Regular feeding on a scale they would have been lucky to receive in the wild had resulted in plump, sturdy, sleek-coated bodies. Already the darker fur on their legs was coming in and their ears, also dark, were nicely pointed and as deeply indicative of prevailing mood as an adult's would be – erect and pointed forward when alert and interested, flattened when feeling aggressive or threatened. Both had beautiful thick brushes, Rufus's white tip particularly impressive.

Their behaviour was an interesting mix. Contact with us had made them extremely tame but inherited instinct often prompted them to behave as if they were still wild – scraping holes to cache voles or scraps of rabbit, for instance, were now routine. They always came rushing to greet us, but if there was something more interesting to do elsewhere, they would be off again after a quick nuzzle, tummy-tickling and a pat or two. They could freely be picked up and petted and, occasionally, we brought them into the kitchen for a romp. When Shuna and Shian could forget their years and dignity, and the cubs had provoked them long enough, great games took place and they rampaged all over the run together. Shuna's ample proportions were irresistible temptation to sharp little teeth and in the end, driven to desperation, she would snarl a warning and the cub would retire discomfited. Respite lasted only a few minutes. Shian the collie, however, had no patience at all and would put up with no nonsense.

So the little foxes seemed to be reasonably happy creatures, enjoying life in captive conditions without getting into too much mischief. Yet Rufus, especially, was showing signs of restlessness. By now, in the wild, both cubs would have been following their mother further afield, learning to hunt for bigger prey and exploring, as they did, more and more of their father's range. The size of that range would have matched the availability of food within it – both prey and a dependable source of carrion. As the dog cubs of a litter become efficient in hunting and more adventurous, they would gradually disperse to find ranges for themselves, or to survive as best they could in a sort of no-man's-land on the perimeters of others. Perhaps our male cub was already feeling the need to wander.

Young females appear to remain within the family unit for some time but are not mated. They may even help with the rearing of their mother's next litter. When the need for a breeding female occurs, maybe after the mother's death, or that of some other vixen, the niche will be filled by the youngster who proves herself to be dominant of the others. Rusty would not experience any of this, of course, though were we to allow it, she and Rufus might well mate when the time was ripe. All the same, she too was restless. Both cubs were digging impressive holes close to the fence, usually working enthusiastically at the same one together, and some of the netting on the fence was being pulled in, as if busy paws were working at it. They wanted out!

Rufus and Rusty came rushing to meet us, noisy greetings demonstrating their usual pleasure in our company. Little did they know! From the beginning we had accustomed them to wearing collars and regularly took them for walks in their enclosure. Now we thought it time to introduce them to the forest and a camping expedition in the van. A large box filled with straw was already in position beneath one of its bunks – a dog would sleep on either side of it to give them confidence. Food was easily taken care of – no smelly pieces of rabbit, or the like, but trouble free tins of dog food that we occasionally fed them when nothing else was available. When we bent to put on the familiar collars they probably decided we were going for a walk, but when each was tucked under an arm and carried out of the run, there was instant and surprised quiet. This turned to panic when we arrived at the van. Rufus fought to free himself and Rusty, evidently thinking that the darkness under my jacket represented a nice safe place in a den, tried to tunnel her way in through its front fastening. Once the struggling pair were safely in their box, however, there was no movement and complete silence. No doubt both were quite overcome by this new experience.

'Right,' said Don as we climbed into our seats. 'Here goes.'

'Do you think they'll be okay?' I asked anxiously.

'Cheer up! We can always play it by ear. There's no law against returning home.'

Don started the engine and let it run for a minute or two. There was no protest from within the fox box. Then he let in the clutch. During the whole of the hour's journey, fast and smooth along the main road, slow and bumpy over a seldom used road in the forest, there was never a squeak from the cubs. Perhaps they, like human babies, were soothed into sleep by the throbbing of an engine. Like the human species as well, this lot sprang to life as soon as we drew up.

As Don jumped out and began gathering together all the materials he would need, scrabbling paws became frantic and the dogs became edgy.

'Take the cubs out and let them see what I'm doing,' he suggested. 'The dogs can come with me.'

So while Don was busy, I sat in the van keeping firm hold of two struggling cubs. Frightened, but curious as well, they soon quietened down and sat watching the party outside with great interest. Don attached two pieces of wire, each about twenty yards long, to a post hammered into the ground and took the other ends out to two separate trees some distance apart. Attached to runners, one wire apiece, the cubs would thus not become entangled together in an exuberant moment but could safely meet at the post. Rope would be demolished in seconds, so we had brought light dog chains to hook on to their collars.

'That's it,' said Don a little while later. 'They should be all right now.'

Rusty and Rufus submitted docilely to being attached to their lines but when they discovered us walking away to the van, they panicked again. Tearing up and down, they fought to meet one another, to get to us, or to free themselves, and each time jerked to a throttling full stop. We walked over with the dogs to reassure them. In a remarkably short time the little foxes settled down. Curiosity replaced fear: this was a new place and the sooner they made it their own the better. They began sniffing over the ground, scraping inquisitively at the soil, exploring for scent. Rufus lifted a leg, Rusty squatted, and then both dropped a scat. They had indeed claimed squatter's rights. In a little while we called Shuna and Shian to sit close to them and retired to the camper for tea.

This must have seemed a strange place to cubs used to the relatively open space of their enclosure. We were parked at the end of a seldom used dead-end road in the middle of a mature modern forest. A larch wood on our right, planted long ago and duly thinned, was a cathedral of light – golden rays breaking through a canopy of gently swaying branches to pattern its floor in sunshine and shade. On the other side, a stand of tall Douglas fir, also thinned, looked cool and inviting in the summer heat. To our young pair, however, both would represent a frightening unknown.

'Let's take them for a walk,' I suggested. 'The dogs can come too.'

'Good idea. That'll work off some energy and then we can put them in their box while we take a look at the badger sett.'

The cubs thought otherwise. This was a new and dangerous place. No way were they going anywhere. Legless, they melted into the ground and refused to budge. Shuna and Shian came to the rescue. No doubt anxious to get away themselves, they nosed the cubs reassuringly, pottered about close by in a casual sort of fashion and kept returning to them with wagging tails and encouraging woofs: come on, it's time to play. Once away, there was no holding the youngsters. They raced ahead with great enthusiasm, nearly pulling us off our feet and frequently winding themselves round our legs. Whenever one stopped to investigate a scent, the other came rushing to help. Two humans being taken for a walk by two fox cubs. In ten minutes we had had enough.

'Do you think we could risk letting them off their leads?' I suggested. 'I don't think they'd wander far from the dogs, or from us for that matter.'

'Hm,' said my husband doubtfully. 'We'll see.'

It was now early evening, and once back at the van, we fed cubs, dogs and ourselves. Then we shut Rufus and Rusty in their box and told the two aggrieved dogs, who expected to come with us, to guard them. If anything awful happened the commotion would probably be loud enough to carry all the way to the badger wood.

There was a badger sett beyond the larch wood which extended over a half mile or so of gently rising ground. We picked our way slowly through soft needles scattered on a bright carpet of grass and over the occasional branch fallen in a recent summer storm. Above our heads, a pale green canopy swayed in the breeze. Next, an old oak wood with restless, rusty brown leaves of many autumns, was difficult to tread quietly. Here we paused to look up at a large buzzard nest built high in a tree, in the fork of two of its branches. Used intermittently over many years it was huge, but this year there was no sign of fresh building or the droppings which would have given away occupancy.

'She's maybe on that ledge again,' I suggested, referring to an impressive outcrop beyond the wood.

'Not tonight,' said Don. 'Badgers first.'

On the top of the knoll stood a group of Scots pine, their dark green needles and pink-brown rugged stems glowing in the evening sunshine. Here, partly among the pine and partly among the leafy oak which spread down a bank to lush meadows beyond, were spread six large holes, deep dug over the years. The badger sett. We pussy-footed the last fifty yards, crept the last few feet inch by inch, then settled into our watching place. Don was crouched in the hollow where a fallen tree straggled torn up roots in the air and I, in camouflage clothing, was close by, a tall straight stem at my back. All we needed now was a badger family.

The yawning cavern that was the main entrance to the sett could be easily seen from our position. There was plenty of evidence of recent activity. Newly scraped out soil and dead bracken had added another layer to the impressive platform at its mouth and on the long slope down into the hole many scratch marks had torn the impacted soil. Judging by the pine needles around it, all scraped aside, riotous badger cub games had been played. Three of the other holes were also visible, two away to our right in the pine wood and the other to our left on a bank of scattered oak and bracken. All was set for an evening's viewing. Meantime we listened to a pair of collared doves coo-ing softly to each other from high in a pine, a blackbird screeching an objection to something we could not see, and two little wrens chattering together from within the fastness of the nearby bracken. Suddenly a woodcock roded high above our heads and we saw it winging swiftly towards the larch wood we had walked through. The familiar signal! Badgers always seemed to emerge shortly after the evening flight of woodcock.

Twenty minutes later came a rustling sound in the dead leaves of the oak wood. I stiffened. Could there be a hole we had not discovered before? It came again and seemed to be uncomfortably close. If it was a badger already out, it would certainly wind us. Now, a long silence. Then more of the mysterious rustling. My spine tingled. Another pause. A gentle scraping sound. Then, all at once, the creature was there. Not a badger, but a large cock pheasant on the top of the oak bank. With a comical air of knowing exactly what he had in mind, he stalked slowly across the main entrance to the sett, paused to scratch the soil at his feet, then continued on towards the pine wood. By now it was getting quite dark, so he was lost to us almost at once, but a sharp fluttering of noisy wings was almost certainly him rising to his roost for the night.

No badgers yet and the light was almost gone. I willed those animals to appear and imagined what we ought to be seeing: the cautious emerging of the boar, or sow, from out of the depths; the careful scenting all around for danger; the call to the cubs below, probably not heard by us, and their appearance, one by one; a busy grooming and scratching of coats; maybe a great rough-and-tumble; then the eventual trotting off into the night to feed in the nearby meadows. With a bit of luck, the cubs would still be too young to follow their parents and we would be treated to cub games around the sett.

Not tonight. Two tawny owls began their territorial hootings, one from the hillside woods to our left, the other some distance behind. Almost time for us to leave, for the entrance to the sett now could only be dimly seen through binoculars. I sensed Don turning towards me, saw ten fingers raised against a pale sky already star-studded, and knew he meant we would give them ten minutes more.

'Strange,' he remarked later as we were walking back through the larch wood. 'They're certainly there.'

'They must have scented us,' I said in disgust.

'We'll come again.'

All was beautifully quiet when we arrived back at camp, the

dogs aware of our coming but knowing they must not bark, the cubs apparently so tired by this new experience that they were out for the count. We let Shuna and Shian out for a few minutes and after a quick cup of tea settled into sleeping bags for a restful night.

'If we've time,' said Don suddenly as I was drifting off, 'we'll take a look at the crags tomorrow. She'll surely be there.'

He meant the buzzard, of course.

In the morning, when we put Rufus and Rusty on to their lines again, we found we had had a visitor during the night. Beside the post to which both were tied was a large scat, certainly not the unimpressive deposit of either of the cubs. They each examined it with great interest and then spent long minutes sniffing at the post where maybe a leg had been lifted. Scent from the camping place must have been picked up by a passing fox, but why had neither the dogs, nor the cubs, reacted? Who knows? But human and dog smell would certainly have scared it away again. Then Rufus lifted his leg too.

'It was their dad,' I said as we gazed at the impressive message.

'Don't be an ass,' was the entirely apt rejoinder.

'I was only joking,' I protested. 'But you never know . . . '

As we sat eating breakfast and watching the cubs working off energy, I thought it was not, after all, an entirely frivolous idea. Glen Darroch was not so far away and dog foxes travel long distances.

'Why don't you take that lot for a walk while I go and look for the buzzard nest?' Don suggested cheerfully, knowing perfectly well what I would prefer to do.

'Thank *you*!' I thought. At the same time I realised it would be quite impossible to leave the cubs on their line unmonitored and probably impracticable to shut them in a box which they could easily wreck if left long enough.

'Okay,' I agreed reluctantly. 'We'd better go in the opposite direction or you'll have two cubs chasing you.'

I called Shuna and Shian to heel, then gathered together two hugely excited cubs, one on each side of me – Don would wait until I was well out of sight before setting out. Off we went along the road we had walked the afternoon before, the dogs trotting soberly beside me, the cubs tearing along. Perhaps they were picking up their own or the stranger's scent. The inevitable happened. Almost at once they crossed leads in front of me, ran behind to meet up with the dogs, and brought me down entangled in snarled up chain. It was both painful and undignified. Don came running to disentangle us all.

'That was a good start,' he mocked. 'Do you want me to come too?'

'No, thank you,' I replied crossly.

I got both cubs on to a really short lead and resigned myself to having to hold the explosive creatures tight. As I strode along to keep up with my charges the dogs kept closely to heel and I could swear, from the smug look on their faces, that they were laughing. Once out of sight of our camping place, I sat on a boulder for a breather. And when the dogs settled beside me and the cubs then edged nearer, to be close to their friends, the idea came back to me. Why not let Rufus and Rusty off their leads? I would keep the dogs to heel and surely the cubs would never stray far from them, especially in a strange place where security, in their presence, would mean everything. Had we not always intended to give them freedom to roam once they were used to the forest? Why not now? Thus I convinced myself it was not a hare-brained scheme.

Rusty was the first to be freed and she was a model of good behaviour. More timid than her brother, she showed no signs of wanting to run away and after a friendly touching of noses with Shuna she seemed to think safety lay in staying close. Rufus surprised me. He realised at once that he was no longer held and, after a preliminary skirmish with his sister, rushed off into the forest – thereby giving me a heart attack. However, he quickly returned and that seemed to bear out my thinking – he would always come to the dogs. From then on we sauntered happily along the road, the dogs to heel, the cubs scampering around them, sometimes stopping to investigate a scent but always rejoining their companions. The peace of early morning, pockets of rising mist from the treetops, little birds chirruping, set the seal on a pleasant dawdle. This is good, I thought. This is easy.

We came to a forest ride which stretched into the distance, away to the right. Here the sun had already arrived and dew was glistening on verdant grass, reeds, and banks of sphagnum moss. Inviting. I knew it led to another forest road which, by means of another ride, would take us back to camp. A circular tour.

Perfect. Let the dogs go free too, I thought. Trained not to roam far into the forest, they would keep to the road and the cubs would follow their example.

'Off you go,' I said to two reproachful animals not used to restraint.

We wandered along in the sunshine, two energetic fox cubs, like small pups with their mothers, romping around the dogs as they did at home. I wondered whether Don had found that buzzard's nest and knew that, if he had, and it was a promising photographic situation, he would already have started to build a hide. It would make an unusual picture, I thought, and I dreamed also of the chicks I would see there.

It was routine, however, to notice a small dark dropping on the top of a boulder not far ahead, not in the centre of the ride but close to the trees some yards away to my left. Better have a look. Yes, it was a scat, and not from a fox either. Roughly half an inch in diameter, twisted, tarry and fresh, it was undoubtedly that of a pine marten. Not surprising. We had martens in the area, but it was always good to know they were about. Still bending to admire the evidence, total silence suddenly struck me. The world was hushed. No dogs had come running to see what I was doing. No fox cubs either. Without rising, I looked hurriedly all around. Not a sign. They had all vanished. Oh god, the cubs!

I was just about to call when I saw the probable cause of it all, a buzzard about two hundred yards ahead. Silhouetted against the bright eastern sky, it was a dark shape hovering on fast-fluttering wings, probably over an unsuspecting vole on the ground below. Quite unconscious of my presence, head down and talons ready, it would drop like a stone when the moment came. As I waited for the bird to act I wondered where those bloody dogs were. Lurking in the vegetation somewhere, watching and waiting too, I imagined. But they were supposed to be with the cubs. When at last I spotted a large golden creature and another, black-and-white, beside it, they were crouched among some reeds on the edge of the forest, but there were no small rufous bodies beside them.

The buzzard suddenly decided there was nothing doing below and came winging over the ride towards me, barely thirty feet up. It passed by the dogs, ignoring them completely, but veered away, uncannily silent, when it saw me ducking. Swooping upwards without a sound, it flew steadily away over the forest.

The cubs? It seemed sensible, for the moment, to sit on a boulder and wait for them to turn up. Surely, any moment, they would come running from the forest to join the dogs and to greet me. I started calling, but only the dogs came trotting over to sit at my feet. Half an hour dragged by – a long time in a fox cub's life – and then, suddenly, Shuna's tail began to wag. Ever so slowly I turned my head to look. At last! Almost hidden by the lower branches of a small sapling, Rusty was sitting with an ingratiating 'smile' on her face. She was scared all right, for when I called her she would not come, though I could see her brush sweeping the ground. I sent Shuna over to reassure her and that did the trick. While the dog stood close, bending to lick her friend, I walked slowly up to the little fox, talking softly all the while. When I picked her up, the little vixen was shaking with excitement and dived into the shelter of my jacket.

Still no Rufus. This made me more anxious. The two cubs were never far apart. Why had he not come running to join his sister? I sent the dogs off to look for him and heard them enthusiastically following a trail among the trees, but they soon gave up and must have lost whatever scent they were following. I waited another half hour, then, thinking it best to leave and hoping that he had retraced his steps to the camper van, set off for base. Rusty, snuggled under my arm, was still sleeping off her fright.

Twenty minutes later, I was expecting a guilty-looking fox cub to creep out from under the van. No such luck, and Don was still away. Should I go back to the ride in case Rufus had made his way back there? Or should I stay put and await developments? I attached Rusty to her line, gave her a drink and a dog biscuit, likewise the dogs, then decided a cup of tea was a good idea before any decisions were made.

The kettle was just coming to the boil when I heard a whistle from the far side of the larch wood. Don was coming. As he emerged from the trees into the clearing, I noticed he was carrying a bundle under his jacket, and as he arrived he pulled a totally unabashed Rufus from within its folds. The young fox did not seem in any way to be put out by his adventure and as soon as he saw his sister he was fighting to join her. We attached him to his line and there were rapturous greetings.

'What on earth happened?' Don asked as I poured his tea.

'Take these over to them before they murder each other,' I said, handing him some more biscuits.

'How did you find him?' I continued, as he climbed in beside me.

'He found me! At the badger sett. The buzzard nest was on the crags, as we thought. Then I went on to the sett. What happened?'

I told him.

'Hm,' he mused. 'I suppose the rascal followed my scent and, of course, the wind happened to be in the right direction. We were lucky.'

That was Rufus's first visit to the badger sett. He was shortly to have an interesting adventure there.

SIX

Midday Madness

SAFELY HOME again that Sunday evening, Rufus and Rusty scampering all over their run to check all was as it should be, I reckoned a quick meal and then to bed was a good idea. Replete and feeling sleepy, I was having a last read when the telephone rang downstairs. A few minutes later Don popped his head round the door.

'That was Torquil,' he said. 'He seems anxious we should go over as soon as possible.'

Torquil McNeill was an old friend whose estate, Craigdarrach, marched with our own forest some miles to the south.

'When?'

'Tomorrow.'

'What does he want, for goodness sake?'

'He wouldn't say. Just laughed and said wait and see.'

Tomorrow was Monday. Don had his I'm-sure-you'll-agree expression on his face and I knew at once he must already have arranged with an understanding boss to sacrifice yet one more day of his total holiday allowance.

'He also wants to take us to one of his badger setts in the evening,' he continued. 'So I thought, since we're having lunch there, we could nip up to Glen Tara first.'

'Is there really a chance of seeing the cat again?' I asked doubtfully, thinking we had had a hectic weekend and a day off would be nice.

'I think so. I just have this feeling we should go right away. As early as possible.'

'Okay,' I agreed with a groan. 'Another short night.'

97

'Early' meant three o'clock in the morning and a tramp in semi-darkness up the Glen of the Eagles. With not a breath of wind, but thick, swirling mist, I imagined mysterious forms against looming rockfaces or stealthily stalking the hillside. By the time we reached our watching place above Glen Tara, it was beginning to clear. The sun was showing a bloodshot rim above the ridge behind us, and over the little lochan pearly curtains were breaking apart to reveal the fairy island of the wild cats. It was magically floating on a bed of cottonwool. The gulls had vanished. Perhaps they had flown to another lochan farther down the glen. The diver was there, though, leading her two chicks in and out of wispy patches where water glistened in the burgeoning light. They were too young to fly as yet, and I wondered how long the mother could protect them from a predatory cat. Companionable croakings, seemingly from the other side of the glen but high above the clouds, were our raven family waking up to a new day.

Then, at last, came the moment we were waiting for – the materialisation of an ancient pine stump. All at once the mist rolled away from it and there it was, tattered and torn, glowing in golden light. It took only a second to realise our luck. As if on cue, kittens came scrambling down the stem and began to scrap over something caught beneath the roots – four wild cat kits all having a squabble. Even with binoculars it was impossible to see what it was all about. Perhaps a small piece of the grouse was caught beneath, and all were hungry. Tattered feathers lay scattered all around and the skeleton remains of the wings could just be seen in the heather. They were hungry. Perhaps, at any moment, the mother might arrive with food.

'You were right!' I whispered.

'Hm,' was all that Don could manage. 'They look settled enough.'

At least we've seen the kittens again, I thought, focusing back on the little group and wondering just how far their mother would have to roam to find prey. Let her come soon! Three kittens were still scrapping, but the fourth had given up and was wandering towards the nearby heather. It sat down on a patch of moss and began cleaning-up operations. With its small tongue, it licked at the tiny patch of white fur on its chest. Then two small paws industriously wiped over ears and cheeks.

Suddenly, all action ceased. No more squabbling. No further whisker washing. Instead, as if on command, four small faces with ears pricked and eyes watchful, were raised to the top of the stump. Seconds later, forepaws on the crumbling rim, head and shoulders raised above it, the wild cat appeared. She had been in the den all the time. Looking warily about and immediately judging it safe, she scrambled her haunches to the top and stood, delicately balanced, looking down on her family. Greedily, we took in those green-yellow eyes caught in the sunshine, the bristling whiskers, the brindled, striped body, silky and sleek, and the gently twitching tail. Somehow we knew it was our last chance. Then, all flowing grace, our cat leapt lithely down and the kittens came scurrying to meet her – time to play, time for fun.

Not a bit of it. The mother ignored them completely, shook herself free, and padded briskly towards the heather. She may have called. That we could not know. But without hesitation, though she never once looked back, the kittens obediently began scurrying to join her. In a few seconds they were safely through the heather and all had disappeared into the cover of the reeds. A moment or two later the cat was parting the stalks on the edge of the pebble beach and, once again, was checking all about her. She crawled out and was followed, one by one, by the kittens. They stood blinking in the bright light and looking not a little dismayed. I wondered if they had ever been there before. The adult sat down, gave her chest a perfunctory lick, then rose with a purposeful air. She stretched her long body, began padding over the gleaming stones towards the water, and four small duplicates of herself trod softly along behind.

'What is she up to?' I whispered.

'Don't know,' replied Don. Then he uttered a startled exclamation. 'Well, I'm damned!'

The cat now stood beside the loch, its shimmering waters caressing her paws. She glanced back at her family, perhaps to give them a call, then stalked straight in. The kittens, running obediently to catch up, found their feet strangely wet, shook them distastefully and retreated to the shore again. What's this? But their mother swam on, never heeding their panic. What to do? They tried again, more cautiously, testing the curious phenomenon which lapped at their feet, sniffing it, patting it.

Then, perhaps noting a fast-disappearing parent, and instinct to follow proving too much, they took the plunge. Charging in, as if that was the only way to overcome fear, they were bowled over again and again by rippling wavelets. But recovering, and finding themselves still alive, the kits discovered that they could swim. Soon they were all paddling briskly after her.

By now I was almost weeping with delight, and Don was mopping his brow.

'I don't believe this,' he said.

It was a brave little armada – a mother cat with kittens, cleaving a steady course across the still waters. Four small washes spread out to merge with the larger one, then drifted away and blended into the placid anonymity of the whole. Safe and sound, the family arrived on the other side. Each kit came gallantly sailing in to tumble ungracefully on to the pebble shore. Five fur coats were vigorously shaken and droplets fell in a sparkling shower. Almost at once the mother led her youngsters off along a narrow, well-worn track.

'Where are they going at this time of the day?' I asked Don, thinking broad daylight was no time for small kittens to be about.

'There's plenty of cover in the forest,' he replied.

And that, indeed, was where they were going. There was a small plantation at the west end of the loch, and there they would certainly find shelter and the kits would learn to hunt voles. We watched the mother vanish into a small burn, which would take her below the fence, and emerge on the other side with the four kittens still in tow. There was a last shaking out of tawny striped coats, a quick licking up, then the mother stalked off into the trees and the kits went romping after her.

We waited for some time, but they did not appear again. All that remained of an awesome experience was a battered old pine stump in the middle of a small island now glowing in warm sunshine, and the black-throated diver, with two chicks still safe, sailing serenely on the still waters. No gulls, no eagle, no ravens – and the wild cat family just a dream? It almost seemed so.

Driving along the forest road an hour and a half later, we thought to the next experience. For sure, it could not possibly match the last. But Torquil was a special person, one of two friends who had a sensible attitude towards foxes and all conservation issues. He ran sheep on the hill in numbers the ecosystem could support and, to make ends meet, had diversified into forestry and tourism as well. He was sure to have something interesting for us.

'It's pointless trying to get rid of foxes,' he would say when irate neighbours accused him of encouraging large numbers of the creatures to breed on his land. 'Others will always come in to fill the empty niche. Anyway, leave them alone and nature soon creates a balance.'

And so it was. There was probably only one breeding den in his part of the glen, though he knew of another high on the moor which was almost certainly used as an alternative by the same pair. Why did numbers not escalate if nothing was done to control them? The answer was simple. No dead sheep or deer grallochs were ever left lying about on his land. They were buried, and though a few might be overlooked by the shepherd it was not in significant numbers. So with bitter weather and lack of feeding, nature's way of controlling the numbers of all wild creatures, there would be few carcases lying around for foxes to scavenge. No surplus food. No surplus foxes. Torquil's, for the most part, survived on rabbits and voles.

'Don't you ever lose lambs?' I once asked him.

'Oh, yes,' he had replied cheerfully. 'Though I'm pretty sure it's those born dead, or those who are sickly and going to die anyway. I don't have many of those, of course!'

Certainly his flocks were meticulously cared for and always looked healthy. Was he too good to be true we had often wondered when we first knew him? However, when he took out an interdict preventing a neighbouring estate owner's shepherd from visiting the dens on Craigdarrach to 'clean' them out, it seemed proof enough that he was not.

Using a short cut on forest roads, we arrived dead on time at the old farm. Even so, Torquil was standing in the yard beside his Land Rover and seemed anxious to be off somewhere at once.

'We'll have coffee later,' he said grumpily, as we jumped down from our van. 'I thought you'd never come.'

'What is it?' Don asked, both of us greatly intrigued.

'Never mind,' he replied, with a smile. 'Jump in.'

As we drove slowly along, I wondered what on earth could be making our normally phlegmatic neighbour so impatient. It had to be some sort of wildlife experience, but the time of day and brilliant sunshine suggested that it would be evidence of it rather than an actual happening. He was not going to tell. We climbed steeply up the rough road in silence, bumping in and out of potholes, skidding over hard-packed ruts, and all the time pushing the old engine to its limit. Then we were rumbling more smoothly along the lower slopes of a long ridge. Crags to our right, with narrow ledges and deep dark clefts, merged at their base with a hillside of scattered large boulders, patches of heather and bracken, and long sweeps of verdant greenery. On the other side of the track, the ground fell more gradually to a loch with small wooded islands dotted in it. On either side, ewes were grazing contentedly, their lambs skipping about close by, all looking in good shape.

'How has the lambing gone?' Don asked.

'Pretty well,' Torquil replied good humouredly, but adding no more.

Even his beloved sheep could not inspire him to talk. Undoubtedly something was up! I nudged Don, who was looking mildly amused, and he shrugged his shoulders. What could be so exciting in this extremely pastoral setting I mused, but as we continued along in comfortable silence I sensed the atmosphere beginning to charge. We were slowing to a crawl and Torquil was looking anxiously down to his left. Then the old Rover shuddered to a halt.

'Of course,' he whispered, conspiratorially. 'They may not be here today.'

How often we had heard that refrain from people anxious to repeat a wildlife experience for us – but it was surprising from our host. He knew what he was about and usually came up with the goods. I noted with interest that we had stopped just where a grassy bank, with heather and stones along the top, would hide the major part of the vehicle. Torquil now lifted himself in his seat, looked anxiously down the hillside, then declared with great satisfaction.

'They're there! Take a look.'

The eye was drawn immediately to a large outcrop about 200 yards down the hillside. Its stark outline, huge dark heather-covered boulders on a hillock of close-cropped grass, could not be missed. We spotted our friend's 'special' at once. A large fox with gleaming coat, gloriously red in the sunshine, was draped elegantly over a flat-topped rock, as if sunbathing was a perfectly normal thing to do in the middle of the day. Its brush extended over the edge and, flicking lazily, seemed to claim ownership of the sombre cavern beneath. A vixen, surely.

'With all these sheep around, too,' I whispered.

'You wait,' chuckled Torquil, quietly.

As he spoke, a rabble of cubs came running, jumping, skidding from the top of the outcrop to nuzzle into the soft belly of their mother. She leapt to her feet angrily, shook them all off, and, as they tore on down the slope, curled herself round and round on her rock, rather as a cat does, tucking her nose into her brindled belly and settling herself once more.

'How do you like that?' asked Torquil, looking pleased with himself.

'In the middle of the day too!' we exclaimed.

The vixen was, indeed, a large one and looked in good condition for an animal with four cubs reared. The youngsters were probably a little over three months old. I wondered what prey species was being used and then remembered a good rabbit population down by the loch. In fact, it was an old warren that the family seemed to be occupying and I reckoned that the heat and a need for exercise had brought the youngsters out in the middle of the day. At their age, it would be hard for their mother to control them.

'Have you ever seen the dog?' I turned to Torquil.

'A couple of times. On my way home late in the evening. He's a large animal too.'

'You feed them too well!' teased Don.

Our friend smiled. 'Keeps the rabbits down,' he said.

Having stayed beside their mother only long enough to discover she would no longer suckle them, the cubs rollicked off again over the grass and into the heather. As usually happens, there seemed to be a dominant one, probably a male, who was leader of the gang. For nearly half an hour, and able to hear their squeals of excitement quite clearly, we watched a puppy-dog game all over the great outcrop, a bunch of healthy young fox cubs chasing after each other through the little paths forged in the heather, skidding down the smooth grass bank beneath, rolling over and over to the bottom as footing was lost, diving into one hole, popping out of another, hiding behind large boulders to pounce on the next one passing, and so on.

'Are cubs usually born in this den?' I asked Torquil.

'Oh no. The vixen has another just below the crags. She brings them down here when they're bigger.'

'Why did you never tell us?' asked Don, curiously.

'Don't know, really. Perhaps because this is the first time I've seen them in the middle of the day.'

Once more the cubs came hurtling down and this time, absorbed in their game, fell in a scrambling heap all over their mother. She leapt to her feet, teeth bared and brush swishing angrily, her kicking, snarling family all falling away from her sides. That was enough. The vixen stretched her beautiful rufous body, leapt gracefully down from her resting place, then led them into the den below. When none had reappeared after ten minutes, I imagined each of the youngsters curled fast asleep at the end of a bunny hole.

'That was terrific,' was all I could say as we relaxed once again into our seats.

Torquil shrugged, but he was obviously well pleased. 'It's what happens when a wild animal has nothing to fear from humans,' he said.

'Have you never had any problems?' asked Don.

'Oh yes. Three years ago, I think it was. I had to shoot a dog fox.'

'What happened?'

'I lost two healthy lambs one night and suspected a fox or a dog from the village. Next evening I sat up to see. It was a fox. He came, quite the thing, as if this was routine, and quickly picked a lamb. I shot him as he sprang. A pity, though. He was a fine animal.'

'What happened after that?' I asked curiously.

'No more trouble and the vixen seemed to manage all right. The cubs would have been quite big by that time, so she must have had a job feeding them. Funny thing is she never took a lamb, so far as I could tell. I haven't lost any this year, and strange to say,' he added with a twinkle, 'nor have my neighbours.'

'That was wonderful,' I enthused, as we drove slowly away. 'It's really nice to see foxes as foxes should be.'

'What do your neighbours think?' asked Don, knowing full

well the attitude of most country folk to this animal.

Torquil smiled. 'Apart from the gentleman who is not allowed near my dens, they tolerate an eccentric.'

Lunch with Torquil and Alison in their gracious old farm house was the usual leisurely affair, with more beautifully prepared food than was good for us and a prolonged period afterwards with coffee and chat in which to recover. It was, in fact, a meal to replace dinner because we would be late, if all went well, coming back from the badgers. There were several setts on the estate, the most active one at this moment being 'at his back door', as our friend put it. We knew it of old, and it would be just a short walk.

There was a graceful birch wood behind the farm and later that evening it was pleasant walking through its gently rustling leaves. Plenty of light, and the sun just setting over the ridge beyond. A great evening, dry and fresh after an earlier shower and, according to Torquil, an excellent chance of seeing the animals. He had built a platform about thirty feet up an old oak tree and from there was an excellent view of most of the holes of the sett. Unless the wind switched right round, there would be little chance of badger noses picking up our scent. There would be just one problem though – there was only room for two on the rickety construction.

'Right,' said Torquil as we arrived. 'There you are. I'll see you later.'

'There's no need for you to go,' Don hurried to assure him. 'You go up with Bridget. I'll stand on the ground against the stem. The wind is okay. They shouldn't scent me.'

'Are you sure?' The farmer seemed doubtful, though he knew that we did a lot of badger watching and should know.

'Honestly.'

So Don plastered himself against the trunk below, hoped he looked like a tree and, quite unintentionally, set in motion an embarrassing event. Torquil and I climbed the scaffolding and everyone settled for a fairly long wait.

Now was the moment to absorb the atmosphere of a place we always loved coming to, and to note signs of activity. The sett was an ancient one, home to badgers for at least a hundred years. On a gently sloping grassy bank, with widely spaced old oaks and patches of bracken taking hold, were the four large holes. All of them looked used. The bank dipped down, quite steeply, towards a shallow burn, and beyond were the farmer's meadows. They were the perfect place for badgers to feed for there his cattle grazed and cow pats would be diligently turned over for earthworms and grubs. Today the tracks along the bank and leading down towards the burn looked well-padded and, as always when we came here, I hoped to catch a badger crossing it. Would it step with care from stone to stone, I wondered, or charge recklessly through the bubbling waters? The inevitable pile of old bedding was heaped outside the main sett entrance. Scraped out by a diligent boar, it looked composed mostly of last season's dead bracken. Impacted soil in front of each hole was scraped and torn apart, and the vegetation over the whole of the bank looked as though an army of badgers was trampling through it. Surely a cub situation.

Time passed agreeably enough and I began to feel a nice tension building in all of us. The light was going and once again from overhead came the urgent give-away 'message' of a roding woodcock: badgers are coming out. Even the valedictory song to the day of a blackbird and a robin seemed a suitable overture to a great badger performance. Any moment, now!

And it happened. Right on cue. A small badger head appeared against the gloomy background of the main entrance. It withdrew for a few seconds then with no further ado the animal climbed out on to the bare soil in front. It was followed at once by two more. Cubs! They were quite large, more than three months old. Apparently lethargic after a long day in a hot den, and not quite sure what to do next, they sat there yawning. Then began a vigorous scratching of coats, already adult, stiff-haired and dark, working away at flanks, bellies, chests and chins. It seemed a routine process, all part of the business of starting the badger 'day'. After five or six minutes, with still no sign of an adult, I wondered whether they were already away hunting for food.

Cleaning-up time over, the young badgers began nosing about in the surrounding vegetation, busily scraping and digging away at the soil. Hungry, maybe, and looking for worms. One wandered off along a path and in the dim distance I could see it squatting. The badger home latrine? Maybe. Then began a desultory scrap which soon erupted into the typical rough-and-tumble of all young things – a boxing, biting and kicking performance accompanied by much grunting and squealing. They started chasing each other along the well-worn tracks, in and out of the holes, as the fox cubs had done at the warren, up and down the bank. The ultimate and blissful climax came when all three, the ringleader probably a young boar, ran right over Don's feet and away down the bank. Torquil nearly fell off the platform trying to see what was happening.

The youngsters all disappeared into the gloom and, alas, it was too dark to see them cross the burn. In a little while, and with no further action, Don looked up and signalled to ask whether we should pack it in and go. To my surprise, Torquil shook his head. He was obviously hoping for sight of the adults and reckoned the light was still good enough. Twenty minutes passed and the birches on the slope above us were losing definition – only their topmost branches, silhouetted against a pale sky, could be seen. Stars were beginning to show. The old oaks were indistinct shapes blending with the vegetation on the bank below. Sound was the faint rustling of branches in the breeze, and a gurgling from the burn. The only badger hole visible was the main one close to us.

I began to feel cold and sleepy. To my horror, I noticed Don's head, only a few feet beneath, nodding forward on to his chest – it had been a long day. He jerked it up again, with a start, and I watched a hand feeling to the trunk behind to steady himself. It seemed a good moment to leave, but when I glanced Torquil's way, he was still obstinately concentrating on the badger hole, obviously unaware of any human dilemmas.

Ten more minutes dragged by. No more badgers appeared, and I was thinking: this is ridiculous. Just as I had made up my mind to tell our enthusiastic friend I had had enough, a large badger came trundling out of the darkness. It was the old boar. His nose was to the ground, perhaps checking on his family, his mind apparently entirely on going home. Then it all happened. The boar paused to test scent on a moss-covered stone, maybe discovered ours, and raised his head to sniff suspiciously. At the same moment Don, obviously asleep, crumpled to the ground with a thump. The badger uttered a surprised grunt and charged into his den. My husband went rolling down the bank and came to rest beside the burn.

Torquil was laughing so hard I thought he would fall off the platform.

'Oh dear!' he spluttered. 'That's badgers for tonight.'

'I must have been tired,' confessed Don, apologetically, as we checked that a free fall to the burn had done no harm.

'Serves you right for getting me up so early this morning,' I teased.

'First thing I knew, I was sitting in a puddle and my feet were in the burn,' he added, shaking the water out of his boots. 'Sorry to muck things up, Torquil.'

As we stumbled along the invisible path back to the farm, our friend suggested a hot drink.

'I think we'd better get home,' I said. 'And I'll take over the driving . . .'

'Thanks for everything,' added Don. 'May we come again? I'd like to try for a photograph of those fox cubs.'

'Of course, but don't leave it too long. They're getting big.'

When at last we arrived home, I put the kettle on while Don, now recovered, went over to feed Rufus and Rusty. He was back within minutes and out of breath.

'The wire's been cut on the gate. I think they're both out.'

'Not again!' I exclaimed.

'I've pulled it together with string,' said Don. 'We'd better check the run.'

We took the dogs with us and all the way across the garden their noses were down. Strange scent? The cubs? Another dog? We walked straight into the enclosure, closed the gate and sent the dogs searching. Shuna knew exactly what was required. After a preliminary sniffing by the gate she ran, nose firmly to the ground, straight for the birches at the top. There she stood wagging her tail and looking upwards. Don beamed the torch there and spotted Rusty. She was huddled against the trunk and obviously frightened.

'I think it was a dog,' said Don, who obviously thought human interference would have made her run for her den.

'Maybe,' I retorted. 'But it did not cut a hole in the gate. Who was it, this time?'

'Don't know. Maybe one of our many admirers!'

Rusty would not be enticed down. Don had first to fetch a ladder. She allowed him to gather her into his arms and once down I comforted her with endearments and dog biscuits while the others did a round of the enclosure. Ten minutes later there was still no Rufus. He had either been scared out, or, finding the hole in the gate, had gone exploring. Once again we were in for the big worry.

On a short summer night, the sky was already becoming pale. Dawn was not far away. It was a good time, with nobody else about, to search. We shut Rusty into the hut the two cubs had occupied when we first had them, and opened the gate of the run. Rufus, if panicked or hungry, might return. I checked the garden and nearby wood and Don did a wider sweep with Shian. We found nothing. On and off all day, whenever we could, we were out calling him, hoping to catch a glimpse, and encouraging the dogs to track him. No luck. By late evening, and nearly dropping, we realised that unless he was holed up somewhere and afraid to move – unlikely with our bold Rufus – he had probably moved further afield.

'He should be all right,' I kept saying over much-needed cups of coffee. 'He's old enough to look after himself.'

'Probably,' agreed Don. 'If he's still alive.'

Not for the first time, I resolved that these would be the last cubs we would ever keep. They were too big a responsibility, and too hard on the emotions.

SEVEN

Flight of the Eagles

MANY HOURS WERE SPENT looking for Rufus with never a glimpse of him. Neighbours were alerted and were helpful, promising to get in touch at once if they saw him. We even baited a live-catcher cage in the hope that he was hungry and would be tempted in. With no luck. Rusty was missing her sibling badly, spending longer hours in her den than usual and showing very little interest in her food. We tried to spend more time with her, often leaving the dogs for company, but she made it quite plain that we were all poor substitutes. A beautiful little vixen now, she had a coat glossy with good health and, to human eyes at least, a cheeky little face that usually had a 'smile' on it – though not at the moment.

A week after the young cub had gone missing, the phone rang early one morning while we were still in bed.

'I think you should come at once,' an Irish voice whispered conspiratorially.

'What on earth's the matter, Paddy?' I asked rather irritably, still half asleep.

'I think your fox cub is here.'

'What?'

'Aye. Come quickly – and quietly.'

Paddy was one of the forest staff and he lived in a lonely cottage some way up Glen Beithe, which was not far away. We threw on some clothes and Don did a quick sprint down to the enclosure to check the cage. Nothing there. Then we were in the car and racing to Paddy's as fast as the rough road would allow. When we arrived, he was standing in his doorway with a finger to his lips and a broad smile across his face.

'Have you caught him, Paddy?' I whispered, after we had tiptoed up the garden path.

'Well, no,' he replied, slowly. 'Sure, he wouldn't come to me anyway. It must be your cub though, the young rascal.'

Without further ado, we followed him along the front wall of his house to the corner and then halted while our guide looked cautiously round. He crept on again, giving urgent hand signals to tell us when to be still and when to advance. I was intrigued. I knew he had a nice sense of the dramatic, but what could Rufus, if indeed it was Rufus, possibly be up to that we had to take these precautions? Our enthusiastic friend disappeared round the far corner and we caught up with him standing quite still beneath the eaves. He motioned us in beside him.

'Don't even bat an eyelid,' he breathed, a twinkle in his eye. 'Look at the sty.'

Constructed of old stone on a level piece of rough ground, it was a ramshackle affair and only a small distance from the cottage. I caught Paddy's excitement, at once. That was certainly our fox. But what on earth was he doing? With might and main, long rufous body stretched tall up one of the walls, it appeared that Rufus was trying to see over the top. His head cocked inquisitively, his ears pricked, and his muzzle twitching, he seemed desperate to discover what was there. But why? Surely the man would be in much more of a tizzy if he had a pig in the sty right now? But Paddy was grinning. I was about to call to the cub, but froze instead. Now the young fox was dancing along the wall, forelegs reaching up, hindlegs hopping sideways, nose lifting eagerly to scent. Any moment, surely, frustration must get the better of him and he would gather his limbs for a leap.

'Good god!' gasped Don, and made to move forward.

'Hold on,' murmured Paddy. 'He won't run away and he can't get in.'

Probably not, I thought, but better catch him while we can. All at once, tuned in to the relative silence of early morning, we could hear the sounds that so fascinated the cub. Soft sucking sounds. Little grunts of pleasure. Competitive squeaks of frustration and anger. An occasional deeper grunt. Good heavens! Paddy's sow was there, after all, and she had piglets. No wonder the young fox was going mad.

Rufus began scraping energetically at the soil close to the wall, perhaps with a tunnel in mind, but stone and rubble built up over many a year would not be shifted. Defeated, he again reached up the sides of the makeshift sty, but could not see over. Then he disappeared round the far end.

'What do you think?' I whispered to Don, assuming this was the moment to get closer.

There was no time to reply. Suddenly, dramatically, Rufus was silhouetted against the pale dawn sky. He was poised on top of the wall, gazing raptly down, evidently totally fascinated by what he saw. At last, he had made it. His brush began to twitch, first tentatively, then rapidly to a frenzy, and then . . . it was all too much. He leapt down, and all hell was let loose. High-pitched squeals from piglets. Deep gruntings and outraged squeals from the mother. Thudding hooves charging as the infuriated sow roared after the cheeky intruder. I imagined the bewildered family scattering everywhere and getting trodden on in the process. There was pandemonium. As we all sprang forward to the rescue, a distinctly ruffled fox cub came bounding up the wall again. On the top, he stood for a moment, looking back over his shoulder – glinting eyes in the risen sun – then slithered ungracefully down the other side and, like a bat out of hell, was instantly away.

'Rufus, Rufie,' we yelled frantically, running to catch up. But he never even paused to look back. Helplessly we watched his lithe long body, brush with white tip flowing out behind, racing easily up the glowing hillside. In and out of bracken and heather he dodged, climbing all the while; in and out of sight, as he slipped behind rocks on an outcrop; glimpsed briefly once more as he trotted below the crags. Then, suddenly, we had lost him. We scrambled over the rough ground, tore as fast as we could up to where he had disappeared, still calling, but would have been better saving our breath. There was little chance now of a youngster gone wild allowing himself to be caught.

'He'll be in a hole somewhere among the rocks,' said Don, as we returned sadly to the cottage.

'Or he doubled back and is down in the wood,' I suggested, remembering the excellent cover in the bottom of the glen.

Either way, there was little point in hanging around. The young fox would go to ground and not be seen again in daylight.

Our badger boar emerging at dusk

His family make their first visit above ground

The old boar struggled desperately in the snare

The female buzzard

Her mate brings food for a hungry youngster

The eagle pair on the eyrie with chicks

Eaglet at six weeks old

The injured eaglet which recovered

Fully feathered eaglet, ready to fly

'It was all my fault,' said Paddy guiltily. 'I'm really sorry.'

'Don't you fret,' I replied. 'We were easily persuaded to watch the fun. Let us know if he returns for more.'

It was with little hope, however, that we travelled home along the rutted road. Rufus had been away too long. Escaped fox cubs were better recaptured at once.

There was one job remaining that could wait no longer and would help to take our minds off Rufus – the visit to the eyrie in the Eagle Glen to check on the young eaglets, especially the one with the wound on its head and an injured wing. The following weekend we were once more parked beside the old pines at the bottom of the glen. Early morning mist, though clinging to the treetops in the gullies, had already cleared ridges and tops. It was sultry, almost ominously still, and I wondered whether the long spell of good weather was going to break. We divided up the gear – anchor iron, mallet and harness, a length of nylon rope, and other bits and pieces – and packed the rucksacks as quickly as possible.

As usual we followed the burn, in the drought a boulder-strewn mockery of itself – puddles not large enough to escape their hollowed beds, and tricklings lazily forging the easiest course towards the loch behind us. The familiar track through the heather was cracked and crumbling beneath our boots, dead roots and dusty peat breaking it apart. At the final dogleg bend, when at last the great cliffs were in sight, they rose out of the haze, a massive and timeless guardian of the eyrie. And seemingly, a long way off. It got steadily warmer and by the time we reached the old marker rock a wall of mist already blotted out the glen behind.

'There's going to be a storm,' I said to Don.

'Maybe,' was his laconic reply. 'Not yet.'

We dumped our baggage and sat on two old friends for a breather – rocks now almost too warm for comfort. Sheep were everywhere on the higher slopes, each ewe with her attendant lamb, and all looking good. In the distance, above Glen Tara, we could see hinds grazing with their calves, no doubt enjoying a cooling breeze on the ridge and some respite from the midges. Of the adult eagles there was no sign, but who knew where they might be? It was easy to miss a dark still bird, even a large one, perched somewhere on the hillside. I felt the usual spooky sense of exposure to gimlet eyes watching our every move. Not that these birds would be bothered too much by a couple of humans walking up the glen at this stage of the breeding process.

'I think we should try to avoid the worst of the bracken,' Don suggested as we sat looking at the climb ahead and the invasive growth on too much of the hillside.

'Do we go by way of the waterfall gully?' I asked, thinking of our heavy loads and the precious camera I was carrying.

''Fraid so. Then we keep below the skyline on the ridge until we are just above the eyrie.'

'Let's get going before it's too hot,' I said.

We followed the course of the waterfall burn most of the way, with detours into the heather when the rock was too steep. It took an hour to reach the narrow gully. Where water usually thundered down the cliffside, and spray clouds fell to wash heather and rock on either side, there was now an apology for a waterfall. The reflected heat from its bared and baking rocks burned our faces and made the sweat pour down our backs. When we paused on the little platform where the tent had been erected so many weeks ago, we marvelled that it had not given way and rolled us down the hill. From time to time we checked for sight of eagle parents, but the field of vision was narrow above our heads and behind was only a hazy backdrop against which no birds of any kind could be seen. Siesta time in the sunshine, perhaps. I wondered what Don would find on the eyrie. Two young eaglets panting in the heat? Only one? Or perhaps none at all and, with luck, some clues as to what might have happened to them.

It was while we were edging our way down through the heather towards the top of the cliff that Don dropped the bombshell.

'I think it should be you today,' he said, ever so casually.

'What?'

'It's time you had a go.'

He was right, of course. We were both licensed each year by the Nature Conservancy Council (now the Scottish Natural Heritage)* to visit an eagle's eyrie and to examine, or photograph,

---

*By law for most predatory and all protected birds a licence is required from the relevant National Authority for the purpose of either examining or photographing the young at the nest.

the young on it, but always in the past it had been Don who did the job. At the last moment, I funked the seemingly precarious business of getting there.

'I've never climbed anything,' I protested, already thinking how wonderful it would be to be close to an eagle chick.

'You'll be all right,' my husband reassured me. 'You don't have to *climb* anything. Just do as I say.'

There was a large boulder right above the eyrie, a few feet in from the edge of the cliff. On its flat top, which was liberally splashed with whitewash, lay the remains of a small red deer calf. This was the rock on which, from farther down the glen, we often saw the cock bird perching. Utterly still he would be, except for occasional preening of a feather or two on breast or back, only his head turning from side to side as he kept sentinel watch on his kingdom. It was also probably the place to which the eagles would bring any items of prey too large to take straight on to the eyrie.

'Right,' said Don briskly as, too quickly, we arrived. 'Let's get to work.'

'Are you sure it's safe?' I wailed.

There was no reply to a silly question. Instead, he knocked in the anchor iron some way up the slope and, threading the rope through its ring, took a length back to the edge of the cliff.

'What do you do with that?' I asked, knowing perfectly well but not reassured and still horribly nervous.

'That goes round my waist . . . so that I can hold you,' he mocked. 'If I can!' he added as an afterthought.

A few minutes later, not greatly comforted, I was strapped into the harness.

'Okay? Right. You're on your own. Don't forget to look at that injured youngster. When you reach the eyrie the rope will go slack. Give it a tug when you want to leave.'

That's great, I thought. I've got to get there first, haven't I? Do I drop straight into it? But I asked no more questions. In too short a time I was on my belly and wriggling, feet first through the heather, towards the cliff edge. Then, too quickly, terra firma seemed to have vanished and my feet and legs were feeling into a bottomless void. Perpendicular rock seemed set on carving my body in half. What now? I was terrified, and stuck. This is it, I thought. I'm not meant for this kind of lark. How do I get the rest of me vertical? Permanently L-shaped, legs dangling, trunk supine, heart thumping, I was not at all sure I would be able to climb back this way either. I tried another huge backwards wriggle, consoling myself with the thought that at least I was held on a rope. There was a horrible moment of 'now there's no going back', and then I found myself over and dangling helplessly.

'Okay?' a voice whispered from above.

'Okay,' I said doubtfully.

Slowly and smoothly Don let me down and I began to think: this is easy, this is fun. Then suddenly I was level with the eyrie. Two things registered in a flash: a pair of solemn eaglets standing against the cliff face, and then, with instant dismay, the distance between the perpendicular rope and their ledge. The rock, smooth and free of vegetation, now sloped quite markedly inwards forming a wonderful weather shelter for the birds, but making the distance between me and their ledge seem enormous. No way was I going to make a nice gentle landing. Not only that: any moment now I would be lowered beyond it.

'Stop!' I yelled without thinking.

The horrendous sound, which would have been instantly recalled had I been able, rebounded from the cliff and echoed round the glen. That was it. There was a startled squawk from one of the eaglets and a hurried, flurried flash of dark body, unpractised wings with white feathering, and a tail also with white on it as it took off. It flew within inches of my swinging body and then had vanished.

'Dear god,' I thought. 'That's done it.'

Any pronounced move on my part might trigger off another premature flight. Another call to Don certainly would. Held still and swinging a little, I had to decide what to do, and quickly. Panic thoughts chased through my mind. Surely that youngster must have been ready to fly; but the other might still have an injured wing and delay a little. Perhaps it would never fly. I must find out. The remaining eaglet had not stirred and was regarding me with dark, inscrutable eyes. Okay, I thought, I'll have a go. I began to swing in as gently as possible towards the ledge.

It took three attempts to bridge the gap and each time, nervously watching the chick who seemed quite unconcerned by my antics, I could not find a foothold. On the last, as I swung away, a small sapling rowan growing from a crack in the face seemed a possible way. Swinging in once more, I managed to grab a branch, got one foot safely lodged on the ledge, then subsided on to my knees.

The precious chick? Slowly, afraid even now that it was preparing to go, I raised my eyes. Human eyes and eaglet's eyes, unwinking, met and were caught in a long moment that seemed never to end. Give it time, I thought. Don't move. Let it get used to you. A few moments later, still not a flicker, but the youngster's eyes were swivelling away to a bluebottle feasting on a bloody scrap. Losing interest almost at once, it stretched its scraggy neck, yawned and began in a matter-of-fact fashion to preen its breast. Thus the tension was eased and as the hooked bill parted the dark feathering and pecked a few more of the remaining pieces of down away I remembered Don telling me that these birds were remarkably tame at this stage. The thought came: could I get closer to this impressive creature, perhaps even touch it?

Instinct told me I could and that this was the moment. Slowly, still on my knees, I began to edge forward – take it gently . . . murmur sweet nothings . . . softly, softly . . . move . . . pause . . . move again . . . don't you dare fly. In an age, talking quietly to the bird all the while, I inched over the white-washed rock and broken twigs, and was there. Oh, good morning, you gorgeous creature! Let's have a proper look at you.

Handsome, gawky, and comical it was. Enormous yellow feet with wicked talons, plusfours above, white merging into brown feathering. A fine black waistcoat with lingering white at its centre. Wings speckled brown, black and white, slightly mantled and giving it a hunched appearance. Yellow cere, and hooked black bill. A regal head already showing promise of the golden crown to come. In fact, a superb young eagle.

Once more, unblinking black eyes were staring into mine. Was there a problem? No going back, anyway. I stretched my fingers cautiously forward, closer and closer to the idiotic creature. Inscrutable eyes held mine – no dawning dismay in them. Ever so slowly my forefinger travelled past its bill, on to the crown, and rested a second or two. Then, ever so gently, I moved it on, down to the neck and round to the breast. No sign of panic. My velvet fingers slid over feathers soft and dark, up and down, up and down, gentling the youngster, willing it not to be alarmed. It seemed the most natural thing in the world to do. Unbelievably smooth, it was, that eaglet waistcoat. Finally, greatly daring and taking care to avoid those deceptively immature feet, I slid my hand over the wings to its back. No flinching. No fear. Okay, let's have a go. Gripping firmly, I slowly lifted the bird on to my knees. Talons, that would one day hold a mountain hare or red deer calf with ease, instantly pierced my breeches and met cringing flesh, but as my fingers crept over the lovely thing I was unaware of any pain.

Now to business. I lifted the bird round on my knees so that its back was to me – great claws grabbing, it released my breeches reluctantly, then clawed again. Very carefully, one hand on each side of it and steadying the plump body, I felt with two fingers to its oxters, testing for swellings or bumps. There was no reaction at all. Then I slid my fingers along the humerus bones to the elbows, flexing the wings apart, testing and making sure there were no swellings there either. Finally, the wings responding to my gentle encouragement, they were spread full-width – only just possible given the available space and limitations of my own puny arms' width – and I flexed them carefully, out and back, making sure there was free movement from shoulder to 'hand'. No restive recoil from this liberty. In fact my friend responded to his medical examination with equanimity and total indifference. Just one more job. I parted the short feathers on the crown to look for a wound. Beautifully healed, it was, the feathering grown in nicely. So far as I could tell, whatever had been wrong was now right. The patient was well and he – I felt sure it was a male – would fly the nest in only a day or two more.

It was a blissful episode which could not be prolonged. My youngster had behaved itself beautifully, but I must not push my luck too far. In any case, Don would be wondering what was going on and if I was in any trouble. I placed the bird carefully back against the smooth cliff face, then withdrew my hands. It stood there, a rather grumpy-looking eaglet, but quite unmoved by its strange experience.

Then it was a matter of shuffling backwards on my knees, inch by inch, to the point of entry. There was just time to note the giant nest all trampled, its sticks broken and covered in whitewash. A swarm of flies buzzed over scraps of rotting flesh;

the two fox cub brushes we had seen from the hide lay forlornly side by side, together with various bones, skins, and the wing of a grouse. Hey! What's that? In a small patch of blaeberry growing at the far end of the shelf there was yet another small brush and a skull. For goodness sake, how many fox cubs had been taken by the eagles?

It was past time to leave. I gave the pre-arranged tug on the rope, eased myself off the broken edge of the eyrie, took one more look at a youngster still regarding me with complete indifference – good luck, beautiful bird – and then was on my way to the grass below.

After a short while, Don came walking quickly down the steep, green slope towards me. He had come by way of the waterfall gully.

'Did you have a good time?' he asked, smiling.

'*Fantastic!* It was the smaller bird that stayed. A male, surely. Its head has mended nicely and the wings seem to be fine.'

'That's great,' responded Don, obviously pleased.

'Did you see the one that flew?' I asked anxiously.

'Don't worry,' he reassured me. 'It landed on a branch in one of the birches. It's still there, but you can't see it from here. The parents will feed it all right. I think we should get on down the hill and out of sight as soon as possible.'

'You're not going to believe this,' I continued. 'There's another fox cub on the eyrie.'

'Really?'

'It was lying at the back of the ledge.'

'So, that's probably three from the same den,' Don speculated. 'Interesting.'

He had brought the rest of the gear along, so we began to divide it up. I opened my rucksack for my share and discovered the camera.

'Damn! I forgot to take any pictures.'

'You must have been having fun.'

'And so', I went on guiltily, 'there are no pictures of fox cub remains or a beautiful eaglet.'

'Never mind. I have some I took a few years back. Remember?'

As we set off down the hill, walking as fast as possible and hoping eagle eyes were watching us go, the sun was suddenly obscured by a huge bank of dirty-looking cloud. The brightness of a moment ago turned to sombre grey. It began to drizzle, and by the time we reached the burn the rain was heavy. At the big dog-leg bend we looked back through the murk. No eagles were to be seen, only their eyrie home just visible against the background of those brooding cliffs. I thought of that splendid shelf with its overhang shelter. At least one chick would be dry in the deluge.

Thunder rumbled. The rain fell in solid sheets. Very soon the burn was transformed, as if by magic, from a miserable trickle into a tumultuous roaring monster. It became much cooler and the van was a welcome sight when, late in the afternoon, we slogged up the last short gradient. I sank into my seat and thought about a hot cup of tea.

'I'd like to take a look at the new planting at Craig Dubh,' said Don as he climbed in. 'Are you too tired?'

'I'm wet. What's so special about it?'

'Nothing, really. One of the men told me there was damage to the trees. It's on the way home. I might as well take a look.'

It was not too far to drive and we were able to take the vehicle right into the forest, almost as far as the clear-felled area which had been replanted. A short walk up a forest ride took us on a gentle slope to the top of a small heather knoll. Once there, a strange sight met our eyes. The new planting, bounded on the far side by mature Norway spruce, looked pretty sorry for itself. The young trees had done well up to a point – a two-foot point. Then something pretty drastic had attacked them. Many were losing their needles, the branches becoming bare. Many were already dead skeletons.

Don did not seem terribly surprised – he was a forester after all. We walked down to look and, thereby, I received a lesson in forestry. Bending down to examine the first sad specimen, I found the bark, close to the ground on its stem, had been nibbled away. The next had the same sort of damage but was already dead.

'Surely that isn't deer damage?' I asked, looking for clues.

'Look at the ground.'

There were lots of little holes – secret holes in among the grass and wild flowers. Small piles of dark, mice-size pellets lay close by. Bingo! The charming little field vole was the culprit, for these were its droppings. The small holes were the entrances to the tunnels which led to their nests. The injury to the trees the result of their nibbling teeth – where the stems were completely ringed, the nutrient sap was cut off and they had died.

'Lesson over?' I joked.

'I reckon,' smiled Don. 'Voles are good for foxes and buzzards, and all. Not good for trees.'

He was right, of course. These little mammals are important to so many wild creatures. It is the most common prey species taken by the fox – the sheep farmer should be pleased for they can eat large quantities of the herbage upon which his sheep survive. Stoats and weasels also hunt them, and most raptors too.

We began the walk back by skirting the new plantation and keeping to the edge of the Norway spruce. It was a seemingly trivial deviation, undertaken largely because we were too lazy to climb the knoll again, but it had a fortunate consequence for the lonely Rusty. We were about halfway along when a tiny sound came from somewhere seemingly deep among the trees. It was a familiar plaintive 'peeping' call.

'That's a deer calf,' I exclaimed.

'Maybe its mother is hanging around until we've gone,' suggested Don.

'I think it's in trouble. Let's have a quick look.'

The rain was still heavy, the canopy above no longer sheltering the ground beneath, its sagging branches allowing through a steady deluge. Already there were deep puddles and all the time the water was building. Could be tricky if there was a creature in trouble. Then, of course, the inevitable. As we turned into the wood and began to home in on the small sound, it was replaced by another, the boiling, bubbling thunder of a lot of water.

'Is there a burn?' I asked Don.

'Yes. Just a little way ahead. There's a culvert under the ride there. We'd better have a look.'

It took only a few minutes, and it was an alarming sight, especially if, somewhere nearby, a small calf was in danger. Debris caught by a fallen branch had built to such an extent that the culvert was blocked and the burn had burst its banks. Water was escaping on either side and flooding into the nearby drains. Something would have to be done. While Don, with much cursing, lowered himself into the rushing waters, I wandered along one of the ditches to see if I could find the calf.

Deeper into the wood, the trees grew closer together and there was more shelter from the rain. The noise of the burn became masked to a mutter and the water in the drain gurgled more pleasantly along. Suddenly I noticed a strange set of prints on the opposite bank. Red deer prints. That's odd, I thought. They seem to be going in both directions, and is it one animal or several? Either way, the deer were more likely to be moving to somewhere else than merely walking up and down a ditch for the fun of it. Then, from nearby, I heard that tiny distress call once again.

Running straight to the spot where the deer prints vanished, I knelt to peer into the ditch. There it was. A red deer calf lying awkwardly in the rising water, one of its hind feet caught in a long straggling root on the side. The body was twisted uncomfortably and the water was perilously close to its head. I raced back for Don.

'See if you can hold it while I try and free that leg,' he said as we stood panting, looking down.

I climbed in as quietly as possible to stand beside the small creature. There was little reaction. Just a token struggle as I slipped a hand beneath its head. I hoped we were not too late. With my other hand I stroked the velvety fur between its ears.

'It's a little hind,' I whispered. 'She's very weak.'

'The foot is badly swollen,' said Don. 'Luckily I've got a knife. Hold her forelegs with your free hand. She might break a bone if she struggles.'

As quickly as possible, and I hoped with no further hurt, he held the injured foot with one hand, cut the offending root with the other, then lifted the unresisting animal to the bank. The little calf lay quietly there, scarcely breathing, a small creature with the russet-tinged, oatmeal-coloured, faintly spotted coat with which it was born. Obviously a late calf. Gently we examined the injured leg and decided there was no fracture, but it was badly sprained at the hoof joint. There would be bruising as well.

'What shall we do with her?' I asked. 'There's no way she'll survive if we leave her here.'

'Judging by those prints, the mother has been up and down trying to get her to follow,' Don surmised.

'Will she still be around?'

'Probably given up by now. That calf has been here for some days. Anyway, the leg needs attention.'

'We'll take her home and see what we can do,' I agreed happily, for I adored both red and roe deer youngsters.

The little one lay still, her eyes closed. She was very thin. Don lifted her into his arms and carried her, dripping water all the way, to the van. I made a nest on my lap with some sacking and held her as comfortably as possible while we drove the rough road home. As we entered the old kitchen, scene of so many similar occasions, the dogs rose from their boxes and I caught a distinctly resigned expression in old Shuna's eyes: another waif for me to nurse. I rumpled an old blanket into a corner and Don carefully laid down our patient. There was little sign of life.

While I made up some lamb feed, he passed a hand over the injured leg.

'I'm sure we're right,' he said. 'There is some movement in the joint, but it is badly bruised and swollen. She won't be able to stand for a while.'

'Let's get some food into her. Then we can decide what to do,' I suggested.

The calf would have none of it. Her nose wrinkled with the familiar milk smell, but when the teat was held against her mouth her lips remained firmly closed. I tried gently to part them, letting milk dribble from the bottle to encourage her, but she was not to be coaxed.

'Try forcing her jaws with one of your hands,' suggested Don. 'I'll hold her still.'

Afraid of hurting the creature, I prised two firmly clamped jaws apart with one hand and placed the teat well over her tongue with the other. She tried to spit it out, but as I held the bottle in place some of the milk oozed in. Gradually the quantity built up. There was a splutter, a strangled gurgle, a bad moment when I thought the animal might choke – then she swallowed. Progress. Nothing I could do, however, would persuade her to suck. This was not her mother. Nevertheless, as the milk continued to spill in, forcing her to swallow, some of it went down and must be reaching where it mattered.

'Let her rest now,' said Don, after about half a pint had disappeared. 'Sleep will do her a world of good.'

Without being told, Shuna curled her ample self around the

youngster in the corner, and while we prepared and ate our meal the calf slept peacefully.

'What shall we call her?' Don asked.

'Gem,' I suggested immediately. 'Because she is one.'

We gave Gem one more meal before we turned in, then stoked up the Aga so that the room would be warm. Already the little creature was sound asleep, the eyes with their silky lashes tight-closed and the bedraggled coat rising regularly up and down with her steady breathing. Shuna was left in charge, but Shian was banished upstairs. One dog would behave itself, two might not.

In the early morning, we were woken by an awful clattering sound. Then silence. What had happened? I rushed down to the kitchen, fearing the worst, and found Gem crashed out on her side with Shuna standing beside her, her tail wagging reassuringly. A chair was lying on the floor and beside it a small table which should have had four saucepans stacked on it. These lay scattered over the floor. The calf must have been trying out her injured leg, we reckoned.

It was a minor setback. Luckily Gem seemed quite unhurt. We comforted her, then Don placed her back on her blanket while I quickly brought her a bottle. This time there was no difficulty. Still famished, she eagerly accepted it and greedily sucked until it was empty. No more problems there. We looked at her leg. The swelling around the joint was down a bit and there seemed to be more movement. It should soon heal. Already she seemed to accept our presence and was less alarmed by the activity all around her.

'She can stay in here for a few days,' I announced firmly, brushing up the droppings and thinking of the damage she could do when fully restored to health. 'Then what?'

'Release eventually, of course,' Don replied. 'Meantime, she'll make a good pal for Rusty.'

'You're joking!'

'Why not? They're both young and healthy. Rusty wouldn't hurt her.'

'I suppose not,' I said doubtfully.

The little red deer calf went from strength to strength and quickly became a 'problem child'. Soon she was 'peeping' for her milk and sucking away as if she had never had any other kind of mother. She had an enormous appetite and quickly recognised me as the source of all things good. At the same time, she was intensely curious. Before long she was hobbling all round the room, poking her delicate nose into anything she found interesting and reaching up to the table with her feet, neck stretched to the limit, in order to see what might be on top. She was a great nibbler. Teacloths, the upholstered seats on the kitchen chairs, and the curtains were all tried for good eating. If the door was left open, she was through it in a flash to explore the rest of the house. Once I caught her trying, on three wobbly legs, to climb the stairs. Within a week both she and we were ready for the great experiment – her rendezvous with Rusty.

Don had already built a small shelter in the fox run which Gem could use if she wanted. By this time, after the rampaging of two young fox cubs, there was little natural cover remaining. One morning we carried her down to the run, slipped through the gate and stood her close beside us. The usual performance with the cub occurred. Rusty came tearing to greet us, but when she saw Gem she skidded to a halt and stood head cocked and tail wagging tentatively. She was used to dogs, however, and maybe this was another. She crept forward again, a few steps at a time. Then, greatly daring, she poked an inquisitive nose towards the calf. For her pains she received a hefty kick. Gem fell over, her bad leg still weak. The vixen fled for her den – two bright eyes, two pricked ears and a twitching nose appeared at once at the entrance.

'It's okay, Rusty,' I called as Don set the calf on her feet. 'She won't bite.' I held out a chocolate biscuit.

This was a treat that could not be resisted. The cub crept slowly back, with many a pause to check on the calf, then snatched the tit-bit and ran off at once, the biscuit held like a bone in her mouth. She disappeared into the den, and there she remained. Once the fox was out of the way, Gem recovered herself. Slowly she began to wander off, sniffing the vegetation and nibbling it. No further alarms occurring, and forgetting us completely, she set off to explore and was soon halfway up the slope to the birches. She seemed quite happy. We waited twenty minutes more, then left them to sort things out for themselves.

You could not say a red deer calf and a red fox, both female, ever became good pals. But two wild creatures came to tolerate one another and occasionally were found to be curled not far apart, enjoying the sunshine. They never played together. Gem's injured leg soon healed, and in spite of the slight limp she was never to lose she skipped about like a young lamb working off high spirits. Often we saw her standing by the fence, her delicate nose lifted to pick up scent from the forest. Perhaps scent she recognised. We would release her as soon as possible, but as she would have taken milk from her mother throughout the coming winter, it would be spring before we could let her go. In the meantime, I planned to bring her a bottle at feeding times and, when she was almost weaned, to top up whatever she could find to graze on with nuts, corn and pellets.

One evening Torquil, our farmer friend, phoned. He wondered if Don would like to attend the meeting of the local fox club as his guest. Now this was an annual event at which local farmers, gamekeepers and shepherds met to declare the number of foxes killed that season and to discuss the fox situation in general. Torquil, disapproving, belonged only because he liked to keep tabs on their activities and to make sure no one thought of visiting his dens. He wondered if Don would find it interesting.

'Will you go?' I asked, curious.

'Might as well see what's going on,' he replied.

'Well, behave yourself,' I chided, knowing how difficult he would find it not to become embroiled, particularly with anyone who was pleased with his own prowess in despatching a number of the 'vermin', as they described the fox.

'Don't worry,' he smiled. 'I've Torquil to think of.'

He came home late, looking tired and thoroughly disgruntled.

'As expected, was it?' I asked sympathetically.

'When we were having a drink afterwards,' he said angrily, 'I told Torquil about the fox cubs on the eyrie. The silly chap had to tell the others.'

'Were they not amazed?' I asked with heavy irony.

'They didn't believe it, and when he told them I had photographs, they said they could easily be faked.'

'There's our reputation, for you,' I said with a rueful laugh.

Over a cup of tea, we talked of eagles and foxes. It seemed ironical that though the one predator helped to control the numbers of the other, thereby making it unlikely that lambs would be predated upon, both were persecuted, the former illegally, because no one was prepared to acknowledge the evidence. I thought back to the morning in the Eagle Glen where, for a few golden moments, I had shared an eagle's eyrie. I wondered if even that awesome experience, with its evidence of young fox cubs taken, could have softened the hearts of the fox hunters.

EIGHT

Drama in the Woods

THE STORM that broke the drought and caused the rivers and burns to fill again also, as prophesied, ended the long spell of good weather. Several weeks of unsettled conditions followed and we found it difficult to fit in all the jobs that still needed to be done. Bird checking had been nicely rounded off by a visit to the Eagle Glen, confirming two eaglets fledged and surviving. Later we had watched the whole family, primaries spread, gliding on summer thermals above the corrie of the foxes, adults catching gold from the sun as they circled, youngsters weaving in and out of parent space, to try out their wings. The deer stalking had now begun and the stags were restless with the approach of the rut. Soon we would be doing some stalking of our own – to see the fun. We still needed to go back to the badger sett near the larch wood, where Rufus and Rusty had had their first experience of camping. On that occasion we had not seen badgers, but it would be good to know now if cubs had been born last spring to the boar and sow, and how they were doing.

Early in September we started for the sett, planning to spend the night out again in order to pay a dusk and dawn visit. This time we did not complicate matters by taking Rusty with us. Once more we parked among the larches. Autumn had yet to touch their foliage – good hard frosts were needed to turn their needles to deepest rust and on into palest yellow. Early evening was working its magic and the setting sun was shafting gold through the branches to light up pale green tops. A red squirrel, on a fragile bough above our heads, balanced easily while revolving a cone in its paws to strip the seed. It took no notice of gawping humans below. The spruce wood across the forest ride was already shadowy beneath its dense canopy, eerily silent in anticipation of the night to come. We gave the dogs a quick run, noted that the wind was right for walking the usual way to the badgers, then set off.

'Looks good,' I whispered to Don when, after a cautious but uneventful approach, we had slipped into the usual watching place.

And it did: hard-packed soil at three of the holes torn by sharp-clawed badger feet; an impressive pile of old bedding building up close to the main entrance; badger paths through the pine trees and heather obviously well-trodden; pine needles and soil scraped where busy badger paws had been digging. Wherever we looked, there were all the signs of a much-used place.

Almost an hour passed, however, and nothing had happened at all, not even a roding woodcock heralding imminent night and, for us, the emergence of badgers at any moment. Wind gently stirred in the branches above. A collared dove – probably one of the pair heard on our last visit – uttered a mournful cadence from a nearby pine. There were no other sounds, not even the almost obligatory owl hooting to its mate. Could the badgers already be out and away feeding? It seemed unlikely – we had come too early for that. I glanced at Don. He shrugged, and with a smile signalled patience.

When the action came at last, it did so with fine dramatic effect. Deep gruntings, impatient and angry, suddenly broke the brooding silence. They came from the big hole in front of us. A badger, at last? Not one but two creatures erupted. A rust-red streak, white cheeks on a pointed, sharp-muzzled face, white-tipped brush flowing out behind was followed by a large dark animal with bristling brindled pelt and white stripes on its face. The badger boar after a fox! The boar snorted with fury as he blundered after the fleeing fox: get the hell out of here! And the fox did just that. He tore along one of the tracks, paused once to glance back at his clumsy pursuer, then, fleet of foot and safe enough now, trotted briskly away through the pine trees. Brock, still breathing fire, plodded gallantly after it. He hadn't a hope, of course, and in a minute or two he came trundling back, still huffing and puffing, to sit by the entrance to the sett. After a prolonged stare into the wood, he rose to his feet, scratched his chin with rasping hind claws, then took himself down again.

Whew! And, surely, surely . . . ! Don was grinning happily. I mouthed the word 'Rufus' and he nodded with a cheerful thumbs-up sign. This cheeky youngster was our missing cub. Pushing his luck a bit, I thought, as the first delight subsided. Foxes do use badger holes, of course, but surely not when badgers are at home? How many badgers, anyway? Perhaps there wasn't a family, and the boar therefore was not too particular about his neighbours – at least, until one over-stepped the mark. We would talk about it later.

There was just a chance we might see Rufus again and perhaps the badger family too. So we stayed on. Another half hour passed slowly. The big hole became more and more difficult to separate from its earthy background and the tracks between the different holes were almost invisible. We had torches, and their glimmer of light would at least enable us to see what was going on within a limited field. Don beamed on to the main hole, transforming it into a cavern of smouldering red light, and I directed my beam to cover the main track along the bank and beyond into the pines.

The boar came cautiously at last, not out of the main hole but from one in the pine wood. He sounded wheezy, snuffling as if he had a heavy cold and grunting to himself as if there were serious matters to consider. First he sniffed carefully over the ground near the hole and a few yards along the track that the fox had taken, then finding nothing to alarm him he padded over to the main entrance. He 'purred' a message to his sow to come on up. And she appeared immediately, glowing weirdly in the strange light, the white stripes on her face startling against the black. She, too, tested the air, then hauled herself out on to the hard-packed platform. Three cubs came tumbling after her – large, one almost as big as the sow, but pelts still juvenile, paler and softer than those of their parents. So! Our badger pair did have a family.

The adults sat scratching their wiry coats. I could almost hear the electricity crackling! The sow, not yet properly woken up, kept yawning and giving us splendid viewing of her impressive dental equipment. The youngsters, bursting with energy and with no thought of dangers lurking, unceremoniously scrambled past and began chasing each other all over the bank. We kept losing them. In and out of our beams they careered, dashing up and down the tracks on the bank, in and out of the holes, unpredictable apparitions appearing from nowhere and everywhere. Then, having lost them for a few minutes, a battle was suddenly in progress on the bank to our left, badger feet churning the fallen oak leaves, badger voices lifted in squeals of excitement and screams of fury. I took my torch cautiously towards the sound, but by the time the beam was in place they had vanished.

The youngsters came soberly back in a few minutes, from a quite different direction. One after the other they trotted towards their parents to settle in a group close by. They seemed to have something on their minds. Steam all worked off, they began scratching chins and bellies in a desultory fashion, kept glancing at the adults expectantly, then yawning again and again when nothing happened. For a while the boar took no notice of all this fuss, but eventually, in his own good time, he rose to his feet, opened his mouth in a cavernous yawn, then lifted his snout to the air. Satisfied there were no problems, and without a backward glance to his family, he set off along the track which would take him to the meadows. The sow rose at once to follow him, and the cubs, expectations at last realised, needed no encouragement. They fell in behind and, in barely a minute, all had passed out of torchlight and into the night. A little while later, a twang from the wire on the fence told us the family was squeezing through. I imagined them busily investigating cow pats and turning them over for succulent beetles and worms.

'Nice little family,' whispered Don.

'Shall we wait for a while?' I asked, thinking of Rufus.

'You bet.'

'What brought him back here, do you think?'

'Chance, I suppose. But once here, he may have remembered something – the camp, the buzzard, finding me at the badger sett. Who knows?'

About half an hour later, when we were getting cold and thinking of leaving, we suddenly heard renewed rustling in the leaves on the bank beside us. A badger? The sound came closer – a mysterious creature in the darkness swishing through the leaves and pausing from time to time to snuffle for scent. Then silence. A long one. Had it gone away? As we waited for a clue, in our own tense silence, our breath passed wraithlike out of monstrous torchlight and dissolved into the darkness above.

Then inch by inch Don swivelled his beam towards the bank, passed over a still dark form, paused, then quickly focused back. It was still there. Not a badger. A fox. Rufus, bolt upright, with ears pricked and nose sniffing inquisitively. Oh my god! Had he picked up our scent and followed it? Could he possibly recognise it after all this time? Or had he already learnt to be suspicious of human presence? Dare we try and make contact?

Luckily we never had to answer that awkward question though, in the long run, it might have been better if we had. I think the cub had just been resting. All at once he rose, stretched his long body, then put his head to the ground. He picked up a rabbit, shook it into place, then with head held low with its weight, walked slowly up the bank. Once only he paused, sending a wary glance our way, then carried on across the mouth of the badger hole and along a track to the pine wood. Just as I was sighing with relief that he would, any second now, be out of torchlight and thus out of temptation's way, he vanished. One second, Rufus. The next, nothing. We waited for twenty minutes but the young fox did not reappear. What had happened to him? Neither did the badgers return to the sett. Not wanting to disturb any of them, we slipped away as quietly as we could.

'Where did he go?' I asked Don, once we had reached the larches.

'Goodness knows. Perhaps he waved a magic wand.'

'Wasn't he looking terrific?'

'He's doing all right. Great to have seen him.'

'The badgers have cubs. Why do you think the boar is tolerating him?'

'We don't know that he is. That might have been Rufus's first visit. If he's using one of their holes,' Don continued, 'it has to be some distance from the main sett.'

'I wish we'd gone to the larch wood when he escaped,' I said. 'We might have caught him then.'

'Surely you'd rather he was free? He's doing well.'

'Of course. But poor Rusty has been so lonely.'

'Perhaps we'll see him again, when we go tomorrow.'

It was intriguing to wonder why the young cub, finding himself free and in a strange world not bounded by a wire fence, had wandered to a part of the forest he had been in before. And why, since this sett was relatively close to home, had he not been back to see Rusty? I remembered a night when demented screechings from the enclosure had us out of bed and running there. We found the little vixen tearing excitedly up and down the fence, but by then the visitor had gone. It could have been Rufus.

We overslept. Instead of badger watching in the morning we visited the sett to try to discover what had happened to Rufus. By full daylight the mystery and magic of the night before had vanished and imaginings as to this or that animal present could not happen. There was no breeze and the wood was full of rising mist that seemed reluctant to leave the tree-tops. Along the track, cobwebs on bracken, filigree threads of amazing strength, caught sunlight to sparkle with a myriad dew drops. Moths of the night fluttered last moments of feeding away and alighted to merge with the corrugated, camouflaging stems of the oaks. Oak leaves were changing to rust, but the pine wood, unchanging, was clad in dark green, a pleasing place of warm sun-dappled stems and boughs. The badger sett, its inhabitants fast asleep, seemed curiously dead, as if it needed the activity of the night before to restore it to life.

We had brought Shuna and Shian with us for exercise and also because their noses often told a tale or two. We skirted the immediate area of the sett, not wishing even mildly to upset the badger family, but returned to the track beyond it in an attempt to discover where Rufus had gone the previous evening. It was not difficult. At the spot where we reckoned he had so dramatically disappeared there was indeed a hole, an old badger hole. A strong smell of fox hung about it and the dogs sniffed enthusiastically at the entrance – for fox, not Rufus of course. Then Shian found an old rabbit bone nearby, and Shuna a scat on a piece of moss. Positive proof. Even with daylight to brush away fantasies of the night before, it was still a fascinating situation. A badger pair with cubs in their traditional sett appeared to be sharing the territory with a fox! If he had been here for some time, our Rufus must be lying pretty low.

'Let's walk down to the meadows,' Don suggested. 'We can go round by the old wall back to the van.'

'And we can see what the badgers were up to last night,' I agreed.

We scrambled down the long slope through the trees and joined the track that the animals used when coming this way. The dogs raced ahead, following scent (fox or badger) first through tall pines then on through the heather, swerving to left and to right and often vanishing altogether. We noticed a scat, still moist and warm, recently deposited on a stone. Did Rufus come this way? As so often happened when we were intent on finding prints and droppings, I was oblivious to all else. Suddenly I realised the dogs had been out of sight for longer than usual. We whistled and called, but neither returned, although they were usually obedient creatures. Then, unexpected and startling, excited barking erupted farther down the slope.

'They were over there a minute ago,' I said, pointing to another lesser used badger track to our left.

'Better go and see.'

We found ourselves among old oak trees, an expanse of meadow now in sight. The narrow path wound in and out of heather, past a couple of birches, and then on to the top of a blaeberry-covered bank. Down the other side we could see the dogs – or rather their wildly waving tails. Close to the fence, heads down in the heather, they ignored our whistles and calls. The yapping became hysterical.

'What the hell . . . ?' said Don.

'They've got something interesting.'

We scrambled down the rocks, and then stood aghast.

'Jesus Christ!' whispered Don. 'Get the dogs away.'

Someone had set a fox snare on the forest fence over one of the tracks the badgers used. It hadn't caught a fox, but a badger. Our badger boar. I hurriedly secured the dogs, quiet now and seeming to know that this was a disaster. The animal had put its head and a forepaw through the loop and then had thrashed around, desperately trying to free itself. The vegetation was all beaten and broken with the frantic attempt. The wire had torn a great gash in the badger's shoulder and chest. There was blood all over its matted and filthy fur. Now he lay quite still and I hoped he was dead.

'Bloody hell!' Don swore angrily again. 'I'll murder that farmer.'

'He's still alive!' I exclaimed, suddenly catching the hint of a twitching nose.

'Can't be.' Don bent closer. 'You're right. Just.'

I wondered how quickly we could get hold of the ranger to put the animal out of its misery, but Don was looking thoughtful.

'He's lost a lot of blood,' he said. 'But I don't think the wound is deep. He might have a chance if we can get him to the vet.'

'I'll fetch the van,' I suggested, 'and bring it round to the gate.'

'Good idea. I'll try and free him. He's too weak to fight.'

The gate, some way along the fence, was at the end of another forest road. It gave easy access to the farmer when he had animals to take to market. The dogs trotted soberly beside me as I climbed the slope to the sett as fast as I could and hurried through the oak wood. Once back at our parking place, we leapt into the van and drove to the field by the other route.

'How is he?' I asked, anxiously.

Don had released the boar with wire-cutters and covered him with his jacket.

'Not good. He's unconscious.'

Gingerly we slid the poor creature into the sack I had brought and carried him to the van. He never stirred and there was no reaction even when we lifted him in beside the dogs.

'George may be able to do something for him,' Don remarked, as he let in the clutch and we drove as fast as possible to the surgery. George was our vet, and a friend who was used to dealing with the battered and bleeding bodies that we brought to him. Luckily he had not yet set out on his rounds. The boar was lifted gently on to the surgery table. He was still alive.

'Poor sod,' the vet exclaimed when he saw the terrible wound. 'Let's have a look at the damage.'

We watched in silence as carefully he checked the torn flesh and listened to heart and lungs.

'I'll do my best,' he pronounced at length. 'But he's lost a lot of blood. Give me a call this evening.'

After what seemed a long day, George reported that he had sewn up the badger and had given him a hefty dose of antibiotic. The animal was still drowsy with the anaesthetic. The next day the news was better. Our boar was out of danger, barring a possible infection. He had even drunk a little milk and gobbled some porridge.

'I can't keep him here,' George had added apologetically. 'I've nowhere large enough, and anyway he's driving my patients mad!'

Within the hour we had fetched our Brock, who was still groggy, and placed him on a bed of straw in the old hut which Rufus and Rusty had used. He grunted and groaned as we carried him, but made no effort to escape. We bolted the cat flap on the outside and reckoned to push his food in that way with a stick – the less contact the boar had with us the better if he was to be released again later. For now, we left him alone to sleep and come to terms with his new surroundings. He was too weak to start rampaging around.

As the days passed the old badger became more and more lively. His wound had healed beautifully and it would not be too long before he could rejoin his family. Meanwhile, we were curious to find out how they were managing and spent a long evening at the badger sett.

At first all seemed normal. The sow emerged ahead of the cubs, did her usual thorough checking to make sure all was well, then called them up. As before, they came scrambling out, full of beans and in a great hurry to work off stored-up energy. A typical badger game ensued, and if the youngsters realised that their father was missing, they certainly did not show it. Their mother, however, was not at all herself. She began a perfunctory grooming, lost interest, then sat staring into the distance, along the path into the pines. She started pottering about near the entrance hole, sniffing for scent on the nearby track but all the while keeping an eye on oak bank and pine wood. It was as if she were expecting the boar to appear at any moment. As he did not, she sat watching the cubs sparring with each other, then restless once more, rose to check all over again. Poor thing! She really did look upset. Eventually, hunger and the needs of her family probably paramount, she led them off towards the meadows. There was no sign of Rufus, but after the badgers had gone we walked over to his hole. In the red glow of the torches, there was no fresh evidence that he was still around, but that was not conclusive. He could easily be there still, especially with no badger boar around to chase him away. We would certainly check once more.

Brock's wound took three weeks to heal and he became

increasingly angry and frustrated with confinement. Soon he would either damage himself again or ruin the hut. George came out to remove the stitches and pronounced him fighting fit and ready to go home.

'How are you going to release him?' he asked curiously while the boar was still charging round the hut even though he had been given a whiff of chloroform.

'Will you use the fox catcher cage?' I asked Don, wondering how we would tempt the animal into it.

'Oh, yes. There won't be a problem.'

'Let me know if you want a hand,' said the vet, eyeing the creature dubiously.

'Don't worry, George,' said Don, laughing. 'After your ministrations, we'll give him time to settle.'

'Good luck to him,' said our friend.

That evening we baited the cage and placed it at the cat flap. Brock was hungry. We slipped both doors apart and he bolted straight in after a piece of rabbit. For a few minutes, as soon as he realised he was caught, he went mad and I was afraid for his newly healed wound. But once we had managed to put the heaving, rolling, drunken cage into the van, we threw a blanket over it and he quietened. During the whole of the journey we heard not a sound.

We could have taken him to the larch wood but were curious to see how he would behave if freed close to the spot where he had been caught. So we drove to the meadows instead. We parked at the gate and checked that no more snares had been set, then lifted a surprised, or stunned, badger down. As soon as the blanket was removed he started charging the sides of the cage again, almost toppling it over. With difficulty we threaded two poles through the wire while the badger tried to grab them in his jaws, then carried him over the long grass.

'For god's sake, let him go,' I puffed.

'Should know where he is by now,' agreed Don.

'Watch your fingers,' I urged as we put him down.

Now for the great moment. The catch was released and the door poked open by means of a long stick. Without hesitation, Brock bolted straight out, stood a moment head raised and snout testing, then trotted purposefully off for the accustomed route through the fence. The last we saw of him he was safely through and making as fast as a badger could up the slope towards the sett.

We paid several visits to the sett after that, to check on his progress. Though he looked a bit odd while the missing fur grew back around the scar of his wound, he seemed to have suffered no long-lasting trauma and family behaviour was soon back to normal. It would have been interesting to see that first meeting between boar and sow but there was no way we could have been there in time. Besides, he probably dived straight down into his home as soon as he arrived, and long before the family was stirring.

This Brock had been lucky. Many are not. Snares set for foxes, in the almost manic offensive against that animal, are the problem. Fox trails are often badger trails too, and the latter are traditional paths to nearby feeding grounds. Snares are set on these to catch the fox but often the badger is the victim. It suffers as well because the fox hunter knows that if a vixen is disturbed at her den she will move her cubs to another. He believes it is often to a badger sett. Without making sure that there is indeed a fox there, he puts terriers down, or stops the holes so that gas can be used. Any badgers there are thus killed. The pressures have been too great. In many Highland areas, healthy populations of these animals have been gradually reduced to non-viable numbers and many setts are now abandoned.

Unfortunately other species are also caught in these snares – red deer and roe, and especially their young, wild cats and hares, otters, even sheep, all undergo a lingering and appalling death. The law requires that snares are checked at least once in each twenty-four hours. This is seldom done, but if it were, there would be at least a chance of saving some of these animals. A friend, disgusted by the number of badgers, otters, and foxes caught on a neighbouring estate, began looking for snares and removing them. He was discovered, of course, but persuaded the owner that if they were left in place, his shepherd should regularly check them. In only a short time, no snares were being set, largely because the task of examining them was too time-consuming. Result? Lamb losses remained constant and showed that all along they had probably been due to poor husbandry. Badger numbers were gradually restored to normal.

We paid several more visits to the badger sett, hoping to see

Rufus again. But we never did. He was a 'wild' fox now and free to run where he would, so we were not greatly concerned. He had looked in excellent condition when last we saw him, so we assumed he was finding and catching prey successfully. That was all that mattered. Moreover, he was now a young male needing to find a niche for himself, probably in another range. He would wander far and wide.

It did not work out like that. One evening, in the middle of October, our friendly neighbour phoned. When Don came through to the kitchen after taking the call, I knew that something was wrong.

'That was Torquil,' he said. 'He has just come home from market. He dropped in at the Tea Room to give Archie a message and saw the body of a fox lying on the bank outside. He thinks it's Rufus.'

'Oh no!'

'I told him we'd go along straight away.'

'Why does he think it's Rufus?' I asked, still hoping that it was not. 'He hasn't seen the cub for months and wouldn't know him.'

As we drove quickly towards Torquil's village I wondered how it had happened. Presumably the fox had been hit by a car and Archie had lifted the body for its skin – taxidermy was his hobby. In autumn and winter so many young foxes are run over on the public highway. The majority are young males no longer tolerated in their home territories and probably looking for pastures new. Quite often it is a deliberate killing, a chasing after an animal bewildered by headlights and run down.

In less than half an hour we were driving up the rough lane that led to Archie's Tea Room. A forlorn bundle of rusty fur lay stretched on the bank opposite the door. The body had been neatly arranged, as though laid out with speculative eye to assess its suitability for stuffing. We stood, shocked and silent, noting the familiar marking, the impudent face, now with bared teeth and lolling tongue, the thick glossy coat and white tip to the tail. Oh, Rufie!

'Bloody drivers!' I swore.

'Was it a driver?' Don mused at last. 'Let's have a look at him. Hold the torch steady.'

The body was still limp and easy to examine. There was no wound, no blood staining the beautiful pelt, and all four legs were seemingly undamaged. It was when Don turned the body over that all was revealed. The left side of the head was badly shattered, the fur all matted with blood, the skin torn. Rufus had been shot.

'That would be terribly risky,' I gasped, jumping to conclusions and assuming the Tea Room proprietor had recovered the body from the road for his own purposes. 'Surely no one would risk using a gun from a car?'

'I don't think it was from a car,' said Don. 'I think we'll go and see Archie.'

'He wouldn't dare, surely? So close to the road . . . '

'Wouldn't he?'

The Tea Room was not in the village but about half a mile down the road. It had been built on to a picturesque old croft house where Archie lived, and stood in a larch wood clearing. Out of business hours the man was a bit of a recluse and, on account of his hobby, suspect to local wildlife enthusiasts. We rang the bell.

'Evening,' he said cheerfully as he opened the door. His face fell at once. Obviously he did not wish to see those mad people from the next village who liked foxes.

'How are you?' he asked, a distinctly wary look in his eyes. 'We're closed.'

'A friend of ours phoned to say there was a dead fox outside the Tea Room and we came over to see it,' Don said. 'We've just had a look. What happened? Was it a car?'

'Well, no. I shot it from the door.'

'Was it after your hens, do you think?' I asked, still polite.

'Well, no. I don't keep them any more.'

'So?'

There was a long pause, as if the man were seeking inspiration.

'You see, this man came to my back door. Said he had travelled a long way and could I give him tea. He saw the fox on the bank. It just sat watching him.'

'Really?' asked Don, with heavy sarcasm.

'Aye. He was surprised it didn't run, so he crept round to the back to warn me. I fetched my gun . . . thought it would make a good skin.'

'Really? Do you usually use a shot gun when you want an unmarked pelt?'

Archie exploded. 'Good riddance to vermin!' he shouted.

'That was our Rufus,' I said angrily. 'Did you think a wild fox would sit still, in broad daylight, asking to be shot? You must have known it was one of ours.'

'I never thought,' he replied, sulkily. 'To me, it was just a fox.'

There was no more to be said. We turned away, and the door slammed. Archie, however, did not get his skin. Don fetched a bag from the van and gently we placed poor Rufus into it. We buried him at home.

NINE

The Call of the Wild

WE WERE EXTREMELY ANGRY that an innocent animal had been killed at least in part because of vindictive feelings towards ourselves. But there was no point in brooding. No law had been broken and nothing could bring back Rufus.

Meanwhile, there was Rusty. In due course she regained her normal high spirits and had probably forgotten her sibling. She had a companion, Gem the calf, but they never became close. She did, however, acquire a small friend, one who did not treat her with the respect a fine fox would expect. One morning I set out for the enclosure to give the calf her milk and paused, as usual, in the middle of our untidy, overgrown shrubbery to peep round a wild rose bush. Something strange was going on. There was no sign of Gem, but close to her den the little vixen, glossy with good health and magnificently rufous, her brush waving from side to side with excitement, was industriously digging a hole. Nothing special about that, of course; foxes are always doing it. But Rusty had an accomplice. Whether she was conscious of him or not, I had no idea, but Mephistopheles, our black-as-night cat, was sitting motionless in the grass close beside her, ears cocked and eyes glued, totally absorbed in the operation. How on earth had the rascal got in?

I managed to edge a few feet forward without either seeing me. The vixen paused, maybe to rest, but her eyes remained firmly fixed on her 'dig'. The cat's tail twitched twice, then was still. The fox picked up the tiny sound of movement and her head cocked. Frantic digging resumed. Puss caught the mood and rose slowly to his feet. With the vixen still scraping – soil flying everywhere – puss sensed the moment had come. With hind legs dithering, he gathered himself to spring. A small field vole came scurrying. Sprung-steel-cat pounced and caught. The surprised vixen recoiled and meekly sat down, resigned. Cat ate mouse slowly and methodically, a wary but mocking eye on the fox, then licked his lips and began cleaning up his face. Rusty lay down and closed her eyes. Arrogant tom, adding insult to injury, began rubbing himself against her face.

So, Rusty and Meph knew one another! It was a strange alliance – a vixen that would allow a domestic cat to steal prey from her and then permit a classic demonstration of feline affection. Eventually the cat curled beside the vixen and both dozed contentedly in the sunshine. How long had this friendship existed? More especially, how was the cat getting into the run? With a possible escape route for Rusty in mind, I walked round the outside of the fence but found nothing to indicate how it was done. Could he have gone over the top? That would mean clawing up a six-foot fence, a scramble across the overhang, and then a big leap down to the ground on the other side. Possible. But what happened when the process had to be reversed and he wanted to get out? We never discovered. He was either performing a monkey act along the underside of the overhang, or making a tremendous leap from one of the birches to the top of the fence – the latter unlikely, for I think Rusty would have followed him.

Mephistopheles became fast friends with both Rusty and Gem and was often to be seen curled comfortably with one or the other. By now the calf had grown into a beautiful little hind, no longer spotted but with a fine brown coat that was thick and polished with good health. Her slender head, with tall twitching ears tuned in to the slightest sound, had the delicate and sensitive appearance typical of the female of that species. Her thickly lashed eyes were luminous and deep brown, and gazed into ours with a gentle trusting look. Now and again, Mephistopheles helped Rusty in her hunt for voles but became more cautious about pinching them after a warning snarl delivered with flattened ears and flashing eyes.

In early October a series of hard frosts triggered off the rut of the red deer in earnest and their mournful roars echoed across forested hillsides and the moorland above. Don wanted some photographs, and so we set off one afternoon with his weird and wonderful new outfit. Last stalking season he had acquired the skin of a stag from the ranger and had dried it out in the sun. Not with a great deal of enthusiasm, I had stitched tapes in strategic places so that the incredible garment could be secured to the human frame. It was designed to smother most of his human scent and, looking like one of the animals, enable him to approach quite close to them. The only thing missing was a handsome head of antlers.

We drove to a point in the forest from which there was easy access to the hill. Don was to stalk eastwards towards a small unplanted knoll where young forest bordered the open hillside. In a hollow on the top, surrounded by heather, he would have an excellent view all round. I was going to a favourite clearing some way to the west.

'A great big stag will get you,' I joked, wrinkling my nose at the overpowering odour.

He topped the disguise with a deerskin cap and grinned.

'It's more how I'm going to get there,' he replied, lugging a heavy rucksack on to the top of the clumsy garment.

'Rather you than me,' I said, with feeling. 'Good luck.'

I watched Humpty Dumpty stagger away with ponderous steps and thought he would topple at any moment. It would be a long, slow walk through pine forest and young spruce before he reached his chosen destination. My route was a narrow gully straight up the hillside. What breeze there was, on this frosty afternoon, drifted in from the north, the direction in which we were both walking, so neither of us should foul up the stalking. All the same, every few minutes I paused to make sure. Gullies are the devil for currents of air doing exactly the opposite to what they are meant to be doing – one second the breeze is nicely in your face as planned, the next it has swooped round a hillock or a wood to chase you from behind, and the deer have vanished without ever you knowing they were there.

In an hour I was close to my clearing and creeping cheerfully along one of the ditches on its edge. So far I had seen no deer, nor even sensed them around. I slipped into the only piece of cover available, hoping that bad stalking had not already frightened any away. My inadequate watching place was the centre space between three spruce saplings about four feet tall. The trees formed the apex of a triangle where two forest rides

Red deer hinds watch us from the ridge

New born red deer calf

Feeding the injured Gem from a bottle

Gem on the way to recovery

Roaring in the red deer rut

Brush for bounty – the ignominious end of a fox

A pair of foxes preparing to mate

Vixen suckling new born cubs

met, and their lower branches, growing thick on the stem, might protect me from sharp-eyed deer so long as I kept still. Scent was another matter. I had to trust that the animals came from the right direction. Crouching behind the thick needles, I hoped my camouflage clothing would do the trick.

The clearing in front must have been left unplanted because of the boggy nature of the ground. At the moment it looked a particularly inviting place, heather-covered, hummocky, dotted with dark boulders and patches of bright green sphagnum, and all sparkling in sunshine on a mantle of frost. Bog myrtle grew thick on the west side, and to the north, where the ground began to rise again towards the far ridge, birches grew on either side of a small burn. To right and left of these lay new forest about ten years old. Each rutting season a stag was often to be seen in the uncluttered space in front of me, energetically defending his harem of hinds.

Nothing happened. A robin, unaware of the new 'tree' beside it, sang an autumn song from the top of one of my spruces. A vole rustled in the vegetation on the nearby ride, foraging for a meal. There were no sounds, however, that suggested the secret movement of deer. More time dragged by. There were no roars from the ridges above – certainly none within the forest. Had the rut come to a premature and sudden ending? Unlikely, I thought.

At long last a tentative grunting came from somewhere near the birches by the burn. It was a curious sound which faded away to nothing, as if the animal had not quite worked himself up to a proper roar. Then silence. Well, I thought, at least I know roughly where you are. Five minutes later, a more prolonged grunting developed into a lugubrious groan which, once again, stuttered away into silence. Not quite ready yet? Next time the stag was much closer. But where? Very slowly I raised my binoculars to the spruce fringing the ride to my right. No dark form was lurking there; no antlers waving in the air gave away a presence hidden by the young trees; no scuffing could be heard as cloven hooves moved slowly through the heather. Nothing, except an occasional meditative grunt. The wretched brute was probably feeding, but I could not see him. Quite close, though. Better keep very still.

In the tense silence which followed, more warblings came from the cheerful robin; no sound from the vole. A hoodie crow squawking overhead, surprised by the human figure below, perhaps had given the game away to my quarry. Then suddenly, with loud and noisy protest, a great concourse of ravens rose from the ridge above and began circling overhead with raucous cries. I counted twenty-two. Must be a gralloch up there, I thought, but what could have disturbed them? Through the glasses I could see no human beings walking or stalking the hill. Perhaps an ardent stag had come charging past to challenge a rival. Whatever had happened, it set all the stags a-roaring and bellowing noisy defiance to the heavens. I could see four restless groups of hinds each with a stag defending and several younger animals challenging. The hills were soon reverberating to the great and troubled sound of the rut.

The cacophony on the ridges prompted my fellow in the forest into action and this time he really let go. A series of grunts, each louder than the last, swelled to a huge bellow which seemed to rend the air asunder. And there he was – standing clear of the birches and on the other side of the clearing, a magnificent ten-pointer cloaked in frosted mud, the steam rising from his flanks and 'dragon-fire' lifting from his nostrils to the icy air. He began tossing his head and pawing the ground. More grunting became another loud roar. Then, head lowered, antlers to the fore, he was charging over the heather – straight towards me! He skidded to a halt some twenty yards away, uttered another anguished bellow, then stood looking fixedly at something a little to my left and over my shoulder. It was quite a moment, for it seemed as if I were staring straight into the fierce brown eyes of a suspicious stag. I hoped he thought I was a tree.

It was not I who held his attention, however, but another stag, a six-pointer poised on the edge of the clearing and dangerously close to scenting me, I guessed. Then I discovered the cause of all the commotion – three hinds in a little group beside the myrtle patch. So that was what it was all about. Coats all glossy and warm in the sunshine, they seemed indifferent to the goings-on close by, meandering slowly into the clearing, nosing the ground, nibbling here and there, lifting beautiful slender heads as they chewed. The younger stag began to move towards them. This was too much. The older let forth another great roar, rose majest-ically on his hindlegs, swivelled round with three ungainly hops, and charged. The six-pointer came charging, too. Both met in a boggy hollow and as antlers clashed and engaged, clink, clatter, clink, mud and water erupted all around them.

That was it! As filthy spray fell back to decorate already muddied coats, the younger stag turned and bolted. He tore headlong through the heather, brushing and crushing the plants in his path, leapt awkwardly over a ditch to cross the ride, then vanished at once into the shelter of young trees. I could hear him crashing about for a few seconds more. The dominant stag had chased after him, but once the younger animal was into the forest he just stood watching. Then apparently satisfied that the interloper had gone, he walked slowly back to his hinds. Perhaps roused, he mounted one of them. With amusement, I watched her chewing cud during the act and noted that none of the hinds had so much as raised her head during the whole stramash. So much for the wooing of two ardent stags! Afterwards, for a while suspicious, the big stag kept lifting his head to sniff, to listen, to grunt a little, but there were no other contenders. To the continuing chorus from the ridges above, the little group slowly wandered off into the forest, and out of sight.

I waited some time for more action, but there was none, and was just planning an unobtrusive exit when a most unlikely sound made me instantly freeze. Surely not? In the middle of the afternoon? Excited squeaking and squealing came from a little way up the ride on my left. Two animals were obviously having a scrap. Two fox cubs? I had to find out. But, wait a minute – better see if they were coming closer. Angry shrieks, a snarl, some pretty fierce growling, and I reckoned one wanted something the other was not going to give up. They were certainly nearer. All of a sudden, two young foxes appeared in the centre of the ride about twenty yards ahead. One had a hare in its jaws and the other was running alongside, trying to pull it away.

Two youngsters, probably males, were out hunting in broad daylight and were either not old enough to know better, or so hungry they were risking it. Quite oblivious of my cowering presence close by, they skidded to a halt on the bank, the one to try and eat, the other to grab a share. Snapping jaws, deep growls, angry chittering. As each of them fought for possession, concerned only with the contest in hand, I greedily took in what I could of two wild creatures behaving naturally. Both were in marvellous condition, well fed and with beautiful coats rufous, thick and shining. I wondered which den had been their original home.

The interlude lasted barely five minutes. The dominant cub pulled away from his sibling, seized the prey once more, then began running on along the ride. The other raced after it. I held my breath, hoped a miracle would happen, and waited for the inevitable. Suddenly and simultaneously, well past me now and downwind, both picked up my scent. First, there was a startled glance in my direction, then in a flash the hare was dropped and both were tearing away. Two streaks of red, both with white tips to their tails, raced back along the ride and into the cover of the plantation. I hoped they would return for their prey later.

I gave them twenty minutes, and myself time to digest the experience. No more deer appeared and there were no roars or grunts to suggest any near. So I set off to meet Don.

'Did you get the picture of the century?' I teased, when eventually I found him sitting on the bank beside the van.

'You bet!' He laughed, ruefully. 'Right away! I heard something brushing in the heather soon after I arrived. Thought it was a stag climbing the knoll in front of me and focused on a likely spot, but nothing happened. I couldn't hear anything and was just going to risk having a look when something made me turn my head. There he was, right behind, and staring straight down at me. Don't know who was most surprised, but I certainly noted a twelve-point head! What a picture! I managed to pick up the other camera and twisted round to focus. Suddenly a "funny" look came into his eyes and I thought ugh, ugh, he's coming for me. I clicked and prepared to dive. He heard the camera, leapt back as if I'd winged him and galloped away.'

'It's a good story,' I mocked.

'It's true!'

'Serves you right,' I laughed. 'Did you have any other adventures?'

'No, and don't be rude. I obviously made a very good stag.'

'Where's the deer skin?' I asked, suddenly noticing it was not on the bank beside us.

'I left it in a ditch,' Don admitted with a grin. 'Reckoned it was too hot and heavy.'

On the way home I told him about the fox cubs. Like me, he

wondered where they had come from, for all the dens in our area had been unsuccessful that spring. Two males looking for pastures new, I guessed.

*

The weeks went by. Don was busy with forestry matters, I was trying to get notes in order and up to date, and autumn, a riot of russets, yellows and browns against the dark green of conifer forest, was fast advancing into winter. It was a time for remembering the season before. Would a superb pair of eaglets survive the hard weather and look for other territories and mates when their parents started to refurbish the eyrie? Where was the wild cat family of Glen Tara and how many kittens would still be alive in the spring? Had the old badger boar learnt a lesson? For sure, he had not, but we would check the meadow fence for snares as often as we could.

Towards the end of December Rusty began to be restless. Most of the day she spent sleeping in her den, but after the evening feed or the walk that we often gave her, she would start running up and down the enclosure fence sniffing for scent and often marking a spot with urine. A call from us and she would come running, but only to chase off again after a brief greeting. We had reached that time of the year when, in the wild, dogs and vixens, which probably pair for life, would be renewing bonds and running together. Was our little vixen looking for a mate? So many foxes are killed in the Highlands and the pressures on the animal are so great that vixens in their first year of life can generally be expected to breed.

Christmas passed and then Hogmanay. The new year ushered itself in with heavy falls of snow which blanketed the whole area in soft whiteness. It was a silent expectant world in the morning, awaiting the first imprint of man but telling many a tale of creatures who had passed in the night. This weather, with short breaks of partial thaw, lasted over the whole month and kept us busy with various wild creatures which had to be rescued and fed. A half-starved buzzard, a hoodie crow needing food and thawing out, and a raven were among the casualties. Gem and Rusty, both in thick winter coats, needed extra feeding to keep out the cold and eagerly awaited our daily visits. Meph spent more time now curled in a basket in our warm kitchen.

One night, at the beginning of February, we were already in bed when we heard, from somewhere close by, as if it had been triggered off by the crackling electricity of intense cold, the piercing scream of a vixen. It echoed over the snow-clad forest and bounced back again from the baffle-board cliffs on the far side of the glen.

'Do you think Rusty wants a mate?' I asked Don.

'Could be,' he replied sleepily, and obviously preferring sleep to a debate on the mating habits of the fox.

A long silence followed, and then the vixen 'spoke' again, a drawn-out wailing call that surely must arouse a dog fox if one were in the vicinity. More silence, that seemed almost to vibrate with the expectancy of both a vixen and two anxious human beings. At last came the reply, from far away: I hear you; I am coming! Two more long screeches rent the air, one from nearby, surely Rusty, the other, almost certainly a dog, much closer than before.

'Sounds promising,' my husband commented, now completely roused. 'Let's try and see what's happening.'

'How?' I asked, knowing it would be difficult to evade the efficient nose of a fox.

'We could put a ladder up one of the pines in the run. Should be high enough if the wind's right. We'll sit on a branch and watch. Tomorrow!'

'Good idea. Could we use torches? There's no moon.'

'The deer torches with filters should do. Anyway, both foxes will be so much in love, they'll never notice.'

By 6 p.m. the next day, muffled in so much thick clothing it was difficult to climb the ladder, we had eased into position along a stout and ancient branch which was clad in the frost that had not lifted all day. Rusty had rushed to greet us, no doubt in joyous anticipation of an extra meal. As we hadn't brought one, she did not try to follow us up the ladder (a distinct possibility well within her powers) but sat gazing at us. Predictably, she soon grew bored and wandered off towards the birches at the top of the run. There we could just make out Gem, standing shadowy and silent.

From high up in our tree, we noticed first the fox prints on either side of the fence. Those on the outside were definitely larger than the more dainty ones within. Encouraging.

However, the dog fox was unlikely to come yet awhile. We settled to listen to the noises of the night. Frost crackled as the temperature changed. Owls kewicked and hooted to each other, and we could see one of them silhouetted on the gable end of our house. Soft rustlings in the vegetation might have been Mephistopheles hunting for voles. An amorous cat yowled on the outskirts of the village. Then, in only twenty minutes, the very sound we were waiting for – a lovelorn vixen lifting her voice to the treetops and sending a compelling message winging into the night. Rusty! We could just pick her out at the gate, every inch alert, waiting for a reply.

It came, and from not far away: I am coming. Then, as we slowly swept the line of the fencing as far as filtered torchlight would go, we spotted a large dog fox dashing across the rough ground between wood and enclosure.

'Keep your torch on Rusty,' whispered Don. 'I'll watch the dog.'

There was really no need for such precautions. Almost at once the two animals came together, one on each side of the gate, and they were certainly unaware of our torches. Muzzle to muzzle, belly to belly, brushes working overtime, they stretched up the intervening mesh and greeted one another rapturously. Each picked out in a glowing red beam against the snow-white background, they chittered excitedly and danced a jig of delight. Then they began chasing up and down the fence, dashing in and out of torchlight, sometimes dark creatures spotlighted against a sparkling fence, sometimes lost against the impenetrable background of tall trees. Their frantic carolling kept us in touch. Rusty, of course, recognised the gate as the place of entry and exit. Perhaps that was why she seemed always to lead the dog there, rolling on to her back to display her brindled charms and screaming an invitation. That little lady certainly knew what it was all about!

I could not help thinking of two waifs rescued in Glen Darroch long ago and the visitor they had had one evening at the run.

'Could that be the dog that came in the spring, the one we thought might be their father?'

'Could be, I suppose,' replied Don doubtfully. He knew my weakness for tidy explanations for everything. 'He's a fine animal anyway.'

This may or may not have been Rusty's father, but the performance went on for nearly twenty minutes. Then, perhaps because his wooing was getting him nowhere, or because he was becoming plain bored, the dog appeared to lose interest. He turned away, lifted his leg to mark the gatepost, then loped off into the forest. Rusty watched him go, sitting rather forlornly on her side of the gate. As he moved out of sight she rose to her feet, stretched her neck to the heavens, and uttered a penetrating shriek. No reply came to her call and maybe this told her that, for the moment, the episode was over. She turned away from the fence and trotted docilely off towards her den without looking back. We gave the dog twenty minutes more, then seeing no sign of his return, descended stiffly to the ground.

'What do you think?' asked Don, as we walked slowly back to the house.

I knew we were both considering the possibility of release.

'We'll have a conference later,' I replied firmly. 'Let's eat first.'

When we had brought the tiny cubs home with us in May, we decided that they would not be released. This was mainly on the grounds that constant contact with us would make them lose all fear of human beings and, wandering perhaps in the neighbourhood, they might hang around the houses in the village. Some were occupied by people who were not kindly disposed towards the fox. There was also the possibility that, never having had to hunt for their food, they might not survive. In fact Rufus, accidentally released, had learned quickly to take care of himself. Rusty, who was now much older than he had been, might not be so successful. Rufus had died because of his acquired trust in humans. Rusty's bonds with them must be even stronger.

On the other hand the little vixen was lonely and only contact with another of her own species would help to alleviate that problem. She was clearly in need of a mate. There seemed to be only two alternatives: let her go now, hoping she would run with her wild mate and learn, by example, how to survive and that human beings were to be avoided at all costs; or find a companion for her, another tame vixen, and hope the two would get on together.

There was another important consideration. If we did release her, suppose after all she was not mated by her eager wooer.

Would she find another? Would she survive if she did not? We knew of two dog foxes in the area that might still be without partners – the one in Glen Darroch whose vixen (Rusty's mother) was killed last season and the one from the Glen of the Eagles whose vixen was killed on the moor of the hen harriers. Both could be roaming the area in search of a mate but, of course, could just as easily have found one by now. It seemed unlikely that there were any fresh territories, for in the Highlands pressures on the animals are so great, either from the fox hunting fraternity or from natural causes such as a shortage of prey or hard winter weather, that these tend to remain constant in number, or indeed become vacant.

'I'd love her to be free,' I said after we had mulled the problem over.

Don nodded. 'I agree. But if we could get her mated before letting her go, she'd have a much better chance.'

'Any ideas?' I asked doubtfully.

'Well. How about getting her used to running on a line again? Then, with a bit of luck, she'll entice her boyfriend into the run. Once the deed is done, we'll let her go.'

'I think we should risk it,' I said.

The nocturnal carollings continued. The dog came visiting each night and Rusty became more and more restless. When I took her for walks, she pulled me along as if we could not get anywhere fast enough, leaving her mark everywhere, on pathways, patches of moss, flat-topped boulders, and generally making sure the fox world knew she wanted a mate. We had to decide exactly when the delicate operation should take place. Vixens are in oestrus for a period of three weeks during the year, but can only be fertilised on three of those days. Previous experience with captive foxes pointed to some time in the third week of February as the vital time. We would have to guess which few days.

On the 15th we began to accustom her to the line. Don rigged a wire from one of the pines behind the den to the post that supported the gate: that would give her reasonable freedom to move. Her customary dog lead was replaced by a chain, for in her present state she would have demolished leather in seconds. We hooked her on for a trial run and waited to see what would happen. It was nearly a disaster. She promptly went mad, almost choked trying to rid herself of the restraining chain on her neck, tore up and down only to be brought up short with a wrench at the end of the line, and eventually became so entangled in nearby dead bracken that we had a job cutting her free.

On the third day, perhaps realising this was a daily routine that had to be endured, she settled. Arriving back from her walk with Shuna and Shian, she sat quietly enough while I attached the offending chain to the wire, and yawned as I stroked and soothed her. After a few more minutes, and with no more signs of panic, she was given a piece of rabbit and then released. By the sixth day, we had stretched the waiting time to an hour, and that evening, when the frosty air shuddered to the hysterical screeching of two foxes, we decided the moment had come. There were other propitious signs. The weather had been good for several weeks, bitterly cold and above all dry. The following evening the moon would be almost full, and so we would be able to see what was happening.

The next day, at five o'clock, we tempted a surprised Gem to a handful of goodies, then led her away to a shed for the night. We hitched an equally surprised Rusty to her wire, for this was much later than usual. She had been fed but I dropped a rabbit for her by the gate. If all went well and we were able to release her, she would at least start life in the wild on a full stomach. Don opened up and we climbed smartly up the ladder and on to a high branch in our pine. The extra rabbit did not really interest Rusty, though she kept sniffing it. The invitingly open gate was another matter. Several times she trotted through and was pulled up short at the limit of the wire. She knew we were in the tree, and kept running back to glance up at us. Then she would dash back to the gate and begin to pant. I felt she was becoming stressed but dared not go down to comfort her – my scent would be all over the place and that dog could turn up at any moment. In the end she seemed to calm down and curled in a small tight ball to doze.

As we sat waiting, the scene below seemed unreal, every detail, every blade of grass, each heather plant, the bracken, all larger than life and finely etched in sparkling frost by the moon. The wire was a silver thread leading to infinity and the open gate a cavernous means to the darkness of the wood beyond. At centre stage lay a seemingly defenceless scrap, abandoned to her fate. I began to suffer the inevitable pangs. Would she be all right? Should we think again?

There was no time for second thoughts. Rusty's head was suddenly raised expectantly. She yawned, rose on all four feet to stretch, then looked long into the wood beyond the gate. She let forth a blood-curdling shriek. A surprised tawny owl, not seen before, lifted off from a silver birch and flew, ghostly and silent, away to the wood. There was no reply from the dog fox, but within the next fifteen minutes the vixen had called three times.

'What do you think?' I breathed at Don, fearful the dog was not coming.

'Give him time,' he whispered back. 'He may be miles away!'

In fact, we did not have long to wait. A few minutes more and we heard the sharp, hoarse yapping of a dog fox. Rusty sprang round to face the sound, ears pricked and lithe body tense. In a second, a shadowy shape, nose close to the ground, came loping out of wooded darkness and into bright moonlight – surely the same handsome fellow we had seen before. Nose checking the trail, he came quickly to the open gate and with no hesitation at all went bounding through towards the vixen. There were squeals of excitement as they met and rapid chitterings as they rose together on hindlegs to box and bite. The dog played eager, sniffing her hindquarters. Submissive, and uttering chirruping sounds of invitation, Rusty rolled over to display her pale grey underparts. She teased him, flirted with him, led him on, all the time her eyes assessing what he would do next. Twice she stood for him, apparently willing, but each time his paw came on to her flank, she snarled and wriggled away.

Preliminaries over, the vixen sauntered away, pretending indifference. The dog, eager and panting, followed at once. The vixen squatted to leave her mark. The dog barged her aside to sniff, scrape, and sniff again. More chirruping sounds from the vixen. Just as I was beginning to wonder if they ever would mate, she suddenly stood and allowed the dog to mount. The act was no different to any other we had seen – a submissive vixen, a dog who knew instinctively what he must do, and a painful locking together, judging by the screams of rage from the vixen.

The deed was done, but we dared not relax. Inextricably tied together and, it must be said, looking extremely uncomfortable, our two foxes stood only twenty yards away. They must not be disturbed. I shivered and wondered how long it would be. Half an hour later they had separated and now stood stretching and yawning in a bored sort of fashion, as if nothing of moment had taken place. Their breath rose from wide-open jaws and lifted away into the frosty air. Then – I could scarcely believe it – they curled amicably close together to sleep. Oh lord! Were we going to be perched in our tree until morning? The moon began to sink behind the wood and the silvery scene would soon fade. We had to know the moment when the dog decided to leave, so that Rusty could be released. I felt for my torch.

Fortunately, perhaps because he would now go hunting, the dog rose to his feet when there was still dappled moonlight through the branches. He yawned mightily, stretched rippling muscles from shoulder to haunches, and glanced briefly at the vixen: come on, it's time to go. Then he trotted towards the gate, picked up the rabbit and carried it off into the wood. Opportunist fox.

'I never thought of that,' chuckled Don. 'It was meant to bring him in, not reward him for behaving properly.'

'Could be good,' I said. 'He'll eat somewhere close and that'll give Rusty a chance to catch up.'

'Too right.'

Rusty was still snoozing. She had lifted her head when the dog left her side, but for the moment she seemed more inclined to recover from her experience than to follow him. Her coat rose and fell in a regular rhythm, though now and again her ears flicked and her limbs twitched as if she was dreaming. For an agonising few minutes we debated the moment to descend: our scent might reach the dog, he might travel too far too quickly. But five minutes later, when the vixen showed signs of stirring, we climbed down and walked quietly towards her. She greeted us with delight, as she always did, but seemed distracted. As we stood patting her gently, there came, loud and clear from the forest, a commanding scream. She leapt to her feet, stood quivering a second, then replied with another. The moment had come. We each gave her a last fond pat, I removed her collar, then slapped her smartly on the rump. For a second she stood quite still looking towards the wood. Then she tore through the gate, over the intervening heather and bracken, and within seconds was out of sight. Rusty had gone.

I heard a sigh of relief beside me and felt the tension ease. We were both grinning like Cheshire cats.

'Oh dear,' I whispered, feeling tearful. 'I hope she'll be all right.'

'Of course she will,' Don said briskly. 'Don't worry.'

But, of course, I would.

TEN

Full Circle

How was Rusty getting on? Where was she? Was she pregnant? These were the questions which kept coming to mind over the next few weeks. For three nights following her mating and release, we heard two foxes calling from somewhere in the glen, but after that the sound was not repeated. For a week we put food by the enclosure each evening, but it was not taken, even by other creatures of the night. Only the hoodie crows benefited. There was never a glimpse of our vixen, in forest, garden, village, or close to the run. She had vanished. It was probably a good sign, for if she had not followed her mate, she would almost certainly have hung around the place that she knew or returned to it when she was hungry.

I tried to imagine what it would be like to be a young vixen whose range had been a small enclosure now having to find a niche for herself in the big wild world of other foxes and other creatures. If she was with the dog, she would learn by example. If she was not, she would lie low at first, skulking for long periods in cover of vegetation or rock. Eventually hunger would begin to bite and finding food would be her prime concern. She would know all about voles for she had often caught them in the run, but rabbits and larger prey would require new skills. The main worry was that she might show herself to human beings and perhaps suffer the same fate as her brother.

Whatever happened, there was nothing we could do except keep an eye open in case she returned. Best to assume she was pregnant and her mate was looking after her. I imagined the two of them running together from dusk to dawn, exploring the bounds of his range and discovering the dens within it. For the vixen this would be an exciting and almost alarming experience. Used to a den made of boulders and turf, a range that included a small wood of birch, a couple of pines, scrub willow, heather and bracken, she was now in a world where everything was on a much larger scale. The forest was huge, and though she had made short forays into it with the dogs and us, it would be quite a different undertaking all on her own, or even with her partner. The hillside above the tree-line would be a vast empty space with what would seem little cover until she learned that rock outcrops often had convenient hiding places beneath huge boulders. She would undoubtedly learn to hunt prey for herself, but the dog fox would also bring her food, and of course, once the cubs were born, he would do all the hunting for a while.

A few weeks before the birthing time the vixen would start a round of the dens. Several would be prepared, loose soil and debris energetically scraped out until she was satisfied all was as it should be, though the final choice would be where instinct told her was right. Now she would become extremely secretive, sleeping there during the day, and when venturing out probably using a different track through the vegetation each time. No scats would be left within the immediate vicinity. As the time drew near for the cubs to be born her mate would start bringing in food. If, by chance, a human being came too close and she felt in any way threatened, she would leave at once for another den. All this behaviour would be instinctive to the young fox.

The agonising thing for us, of course, was that we could only guess at what was happening. The proof of our little vixen's survival and success could come only later, when we did our usual checking of the dens and perhaps discovered the one that she was using.

In the middle of April there was a setback. For two days a blizzard raged – something not uncommon in the Highlands at this time of the year. There was a lot of snow and huge drifts built up. It was followed by a week of hard frosts when food, for all wild creatures in the wood and out on bare hillsides, would be difficult to find. It was at this time that Rusty would have been due to give birth – the gestation period for vixens being around 52 days. She would now be completely dependent on her mate and we wondered if he was finding prey enough. We thought, as well, of eagle and peregrine hens crouching stoically over their eggs in the bitter blast.

Poor Rusty. Would she survive? Three long weeks she would spend in the den suckling, cleaning and keeping snug and warm three, four, or five cubs each weighing between three and four ounces, with soft dark chocolate-coloured fur, some with white tips to the ends of stringy little tails, all blind, and whose only instinct would be to eat and sleep on a regular and frequent basis. Their mother would leave them only to relieve herself, to stretch stiff limbs, and to collect food from her mate when he brought it to the den. She would grow lean and scruffy-looking, and her teats would grow sore with constant use.

During the whole of this early period the vixen would not allow the dog anywhere near his family and certainly not down into the den. This he would take entirely for granted. When he brought in prey, he would call to her with little chirruping sounds, then drop it at her feet. She would snatch it greedily without ceremony or greeting and immediately carry it back to the den. Foxes usually pair for life, and are sociable creatures within the family group, but this would not be the occasion for friendly greetings. Once the cubs began to struggle out of the den to explore the world outside, usually from about five weeks old, he would have contact with his young family.

Fortunately the spell of bad weather lasted only a short time and balmy spring sunshine followed. By the end of the month we were getting itchy feet and were more and more anxious to know how our vixen had fared. A little earlier than usual, we started on the routine checking of all the traditional dens to discover which were in use. Each had to be viewed from afar through binoculars, making sure no sound or scenting of our presence could occur. By now, after three weeks or so, the vixens would be leaving the dens for short periods to sleep nearby and rest from the demanding attentions of the cubs. Shortly, too, they would begin hunting for prey again. We hoped for a glimpse of one lying curled in a favourite place close by, or even prowling in the nearby vegetation. On a bare and beaten patch not far from the den would be a scattering of bones and fur, remains of the family prey. That was the evidence we would be looking for at this stage.

Time passed and many miles were covered in a systematic

round of the dens. There was no sign of activity at the two in the Glen of the Eagles, in itself not especially significant for the vixen which might have replaced last year's fatality could easily be using an alternative one in nearby forest or out on the moor. It was encouraging to see, just visible above that huge pile of sticks on the cliff, the chestnut gold head of the eagle hen. With hatching time not too far away, she would be sitting tight on her two mottled eggs. Later in the season, if all went well, we might be lucky enough to see the whole family gliding on thermals above the glen, practising eagle manoeuvres over its cliffs and wooded hillsides.

Glen Tara was a disaster. Of the two dens there, one was not in use but the other exhibited all the familiar signs of a visit from the fox hunters – heavily trampled vegetation, soil ravaged and torn at the entrance where terriers had gone in to do their work, and a dead vixen, minus her brush, hanging on the branches of a nearby birch. We lifted her gently down and built her a burial cairn in the middle of a patch of heather. At the den itself, no faint squeaks could be heard and, as far as could be discovered, there were no small cubs to be rescued.

We checked all the dens we knew in the forests surrounding us and among rocky escarpments high on the moors above. None was in use and, exploring a bit to make sure, we came across no new ones. It would seem there were no vixens breeding in the area and, even more alarming, there was a strong possibility that Rusty was dead. What could be the reason for this sorry state of affairs? Could the bad spell of weather in April have caused vixens to abandon their cubs and seek the bare needs of their own survival? Were the fox hunters too successful last year, and were no vixens coming in from other ranges to replace those despatched then? There were a number of possibilities but, in the absence of precise evidence by early June, we could only guess the reason.

'There's only Glen Darroch left,' I said despairingly to Don one morning at breakfast, last year's devastation in mind.

'If she's still alive!'

There was only one den we knew of in that glen and it was where Rusty had been born and where her mother and siblings had been killed. There were scattered hideaways out on the peat moors above but we had already checked there. With its doomful associations it was the last place we could have wished for Rusty. I felt childishly aggrieved that, if she were there, nature had not fed into her foxy computer mind an instinct to avoid it. Anyway, the fox hunters would surely have done their work by now.

'We'll go on Saturday,' said Don.

'Why don't we walk the ridge? We would have a better view of the den from up there,' I suggested.

'Good idea.'

So the following weekend, on a typical cool Highland evening at the end of a hot and humid day, we packed rucksacks with the bare essentials for a night out and set off. The van was left at the bottom of the glen and with very mixed feelings we began the steep, short climb that would take us to the ridge. Once there, it was nice easy walking on a wonderfully bright evening cold enough to discourage the midges. Our boots swished comfortably through heather trails made by the deer and we spoke little. There were soothing sounds of meadow pipit and wheatear, and the noisy squabblings of a jay family in the forest below. With the breeze in our faces, there was no warning of our approach to a small group of hinds ahead. Completely unaware of our presence, they were browsing a last meal of the day on young heather shoots and their jaws worked rhythmically as they chewed. Coats were patchy and rough-looking in the change to summer pelage but were glowing warmly pink in the setting sun. As we came slowly nearer, the matriarch at last discovered us. She hesitated, knowing well it was the close season and there was no danger, then began a gentle amble up the hillside. The others followed, sauntering slowly away with many a pause to look back or even to graze a mouthful. Eventually they all disappeared over the other side of the ridge.

Within an hour we were standing just below the skyline and gazing down over the familiar ravaged landscape of a year ago.

'Let's have a look at the den,' I said, hoping, even at this distance, it would give us a clue.

In fact it was still just out of sight, hidden beneath the huge outcrop that sheltered it. Only one change was evident in the general scene. A small landslip, no doubt triggered off by heavy rain and newly born waterfalls cascading down the hillside, had dried out and was now an impressive scree-fall tumbling to the forest below. The rest was the rock-strewn, gully-scored, heather-patched hillside of old, its few skeleton trees even more stricken-looking than before. Below the forest fence conifers, larch, pine and spruce, planted to match the contours of the hill and now mature and gracious trees, were pleasant relief in almost desert conditions.

'Let's get down there,' said Don. 'The light will begin to go in an hour or so.'

Alert for any change of wind direction which would give us away, or for a sighting of a fox already quartering the slopes below, we made our way slowly down to our watching place. Before long we were in position about 150 yards from the den, but still higher on the hillside. We had boulders for background and the breeze was safely from the top of the glen.

'What do you think?' I asked Don as we anxiously trained binoculars first on the monstrous rocks which guarded the den and then on the yawning cavern beneath.

'What do *you* think?' he teased after a few moments.

Not only had this den been used, it was obviously still in use. At four to five weeks, the vixen would have started to wean her cubs, bringing them small scraps of flesh to chew on and suckling them less and less. At the same time she would be encouraging them to climb out of the den to discover the world outside. These cubs should now have reached this stage and fresh prey remains be scattered about haphazardly. There would be padded down grass all around the den, well-worn trails in the heather beyond, and soil at the rock entrance all torn and scraped by busy feet. As growing and often hungry cubs, they would battle fiercely for any prey brought in by either of the parents and then play strenuous puppy games to work off energy until they were ready to sleep. All the classic signs were splendidly present. A fox family was in residence. But was the vixen Rusty? I was desperate to know.

'Looks promising,' commented Don.

'If only it could be Rusty!'

We settled to wait, comfortable in the knowledge that our camouflage clothing turned us into patches of green and brown against the surrounding lichen and heather-patched boulders. Unchanging magnificence, the far ridge already in deepest shadow, dark mountains in the west thrusting rugged summits to welcome the setting sun, the sky a fiery red and pink, all prompted superstitious stirrings of alarm that the disaster of last season might still be repeated. It ought not to matter, of course, which vixen died, but it would hit the harder if it was Rusty.

Time passed too quickly, with the certainty of darkness soon to come. Thunderclouds began to build in the west and I realised, with dismay, that the wind might change direction and perhaps give us away. The sun, firing parting shafts of gold and red, disappeared behind massing cumulus and the sun-dappled glen below faded quickly into muted shades of green and grey. Rocks above the den were weirdly silhouetted sentinels, deepest black against the angry sky. Below their lowering shapes, the unfathomable depths of the cavern loomed darkly. Still no movement there and soon all we would be able to see might be the small shapes of dark never-still cubs against the larger one of their shadowy mother. Certainly we would not be able to identify Rusty definitely. I noticed the piece of wire which was propped against the forest fence and remembered two small waifs dragged to safety last year.

'Let's hope there'll be something to see in the morning,' said Don, turning at last to unpack his rucksack.

'Give it a minute or two,' I pleaded. 'I can still see the den through the binoculars.'

Don shrugged. He was focused on the hillside immediately below us. Suddenly I sensed him stiffen.

'Keep quite still,' he whispered.

In a second I had it. A streak of tawny fur was struggling along the bottom of a ditch in the forest. A fox! This must be the means by which it would pass under the fence and on to the open hillside. It was moving slowly, stumbling a bit, and appeared to be holding something awkward in its mouth. Then it disappeared. Was it not, after all, going under the fence? A second or two later, under and through, the animal was climbing the bank. I could see all of it clearly – head held high and alert, hare hanging from jaws, long rufous body, brush flowing out behind. It was small and dainty. For sure, a vixen. As she stood motionless and beautiful, 'pointing' in the direction of the den, I knew without doubt it was Rusty.

'Oh my god!' I whispered.

'Hush,' hissed Don, but then he relented. 'Just like her,' he added with a broad smile.

'Of course it's Rusty!'

Don had with him a photo he had taken just before we released her. We looked at it now, and in one glorious moment knew that this was indeed our little vixen, and she was very much alive. What was more, the only place to which she could be taking that hare was the den we were watching. So these cubs were certainly hers. The next few minutes were agonising. Which way would she go? Would she scent us, drop her prize, and run away? The vixen stood staring for long seconds, checking the way ahead. She dropped the hare, tested the air, then relaxed. She uttered a long, warbling kind of a call: I am coming. Then she picked up the animal at her feet and with some difficulty began stalking through the heather. Twenty yards from home, she dropped the hare again and stood quite still. I imagined a soft, chirruping call of invitation: come and get it. And they did. Three cubs came tumbling out, barging, scrapping, scrambling to be the first to reach her and to grab hold of her prey.

'The little darling,' I whispered. 'She's made it!'

'Looks like it,' admitted Don. 'Thank goodness.'

The scene below was clear enough through binoculars, and the action as you might expect. While the mother sat complacently by, cleaning up her coat and occasionally glancing at her family, they all squabbled for a share of the loot, though we could not hear the growling, snarling and snickering that would be going on. They looked fighting fit and as full of mischief as any young cubs could be. One was larger than the others, probably male, and the only one with a white tip to its tail. Adult marking was almost complete though the coats still looked soft and woolly. Perhaps we would see them all more clearly with better light in the morning.

We were so absorbed with the action at the den that when a faint breath of air touched my left cheek I did not at once think it significant. Then it dawned on me. The wind, such as it was, had shifted a few points westward, as if moving round to a more southerly direction. It would soon take our scent to the den.

Don was frowning. 'Hell!' he said quietly.

'We daren't move,' I whispered, stating the obvious.

'Let's ease back among the rocks under the overhang behind us and hope for the best.'

With clouds massing in the west, the light had almost gone.

We crept back into the darkness of our shelter and slipped quietly into sleeping bags, but not to much sleep. It was a cold and restless night, what was left of it. There was a rumble or two from a far off storm but no sound of heavy rain beating on the rocks around us. When at last soft light etched the eastern ridge with promise of dawn, we crawled out into our watching place and cautiously sniffed the air. Good. No breeze at all that mattered. The menacing clouds had long rolled away and dampness from a shower in the night mantled the nearby vegetation and rock, making them shimmer fresh and clean. Without doubt, as the temperature rose, the midges would get to work. An hour went by during which the sky turned pink and gold and the light steadily improved. The mysterious unseen world beyond took on shape and colour and all our attention was on the yawning cavern of the fox den.

Nothing whatever happened. We would have expected the cubs to be out for a final airing before spending the long hours of bright daylight in the den. But they were not. Their mother might already have called them down, but it seemed unlikely that youngsters as lively as these would be in a hurry to obey. The sun rose above the far ridge and a mountain blackbird greeted the day. Wheatear and meadow pipit began flitting all over the hillside, collecting food for their young. But of the fox family, there was no sign. The mouth of the den remained blank, the cub playground empty. It seemed as if the events of the previous evening had been a dream.

The glen was soon bathed in warm sunshine. Mist climbed the hillsides and dispersed into an azure sky. The early sheen on rock and vegetation soon dried out and the familiar arid splendour was once more shimmering in the heat. But there were no foxes. By mid-morning it was unlikely we would see anything of them and we gave up.

'We'll go by the ridge again,' was Don's suggestion, when at last we turned reluctantly for home.

'Who knows?' I joked. 'We might meet a fox.'

'Of course, she may still be in the den,' Don said doubtfully. 'But I have this horrible feeling she's gone.'

'Me, too,' I agreed. 'It must have been the change in the wind. Perhaps she went hunting again and picked up our scent.'

'It's possible.'

The thought of our Rusty perhaps only yards away during the night was kind of eerie.

'Surely it would be difficult for her to move the cubs? They're so big,' I persisted, having visions of the little vixen carrying each heavy youngster in her mouth across the rough hillside to a den some distance away.

'They're old enough to follow now. Don't worry. She's a survivor and seems to have done all the things a vixen should do.'

'Why would that den have been left alone?' I continued, still thinking of last year and the fox hunters.

'Don't know. One thing, though. Rusty may have been disturbed at another one, by chance, and then brought her cubs here. Perhaps the men had been here already and thought the den not in use.'

It was a nice idea. I walked more happily through the heather, enjoying the sunshine and revelling in the comfortable thought that Rusty was alive, had produced a family, and seemed to be doing well.

When we reached the end of the ridge, contentment was rudely shattered. Just as we were beginning the descent, the dull report of a shotgun, fired not far way, instantly jerked us to a halt. A pair of hoodie crows rose above the forest with raucous cries.

'Oh my god!' I wailed.

The awful possibility of Rusty's death and that of the cubs drove all common sense away.

'Was it close to the den, do you think?' I asked anxiously.

'Steady on,' said Don. 'It's probably someone out after hares or hoodies.'

'I hope you're right.'

We scanned every inch of the hillside but saw no one. In any case, whoever it was could easily be within the cover of the trees.

'What can we do?' I asked impatiently.

'Not much,' replied Don. 'If they're going to the den, there's no way we could reach it before they do. Wonder why they're so late in the season with this one.'

We scrambled down the gully as fast as we could, anxious to know the worst. The fox hunter's van was parked beside ours. My imagination ran riot: a sinister group of men with guns and terriers stalking up the glen; the doomed den; a terrified vixen, our Rusty, and her cubs cowering within; carnage with guns and terriers; pathetic bundles of fur tossed into the heather. I felt sick.

'There's just one thing,' said Don thoughtfully as we reached the bottom. 'Remember. We didn't see the cubs this morning. Rusty may have taken them to another den.'

'Could we not have done more to protect her?' I asked.

'No – and you know it,' Don replied gently. 'Rusty has to make out for herself now.'

Epilogue

WE never discovered what happened to Rusty and that, too often, is the norm when an animal is released back into the wild. She did not reappear at the den with her family. Neither did she seem to be sheltering in any of the other dens we knew. We could only hope she was using one that we had so far not discovered.

The following season did not produce any miracles either. There was no evidence of her death, but news of it would be unlikely to reach us. She had vanished as if she had never been and our only comfort was the thought that for a little while she had been free to be a proper little vixen, roaming the hills of her range, running with her mate and producing a fine family of cubs. Perhaps that had been better than confinement in however well-devised circumstances. It was impossible to be sure.

APPENDIX

Wild Mammals (Protection) Bill

Rufus and Rusty were orphan cubs found in the den of their birth, abandoned by the fox hunters. The fate of their mother and siblings was similar to that of countless fox families, each spring in the Highlands of Scotland and in many other parts of the country. In the Highlands, where fox hunting on horseback is impracticable because of the terrain, the traditional method of fox control is to send terriers into the den to bolt the vixen, who defends her young to the last desperate moment, and then flees. She is shot at the entrance and her terrified cubs are either despatched by the terriers or left to die of starvation. Other methods include snaring, lamping, and gassing, and there are at least two packs of hounds in the Highlands which the hunters follow on foot. All these methods, with the exception of lamping at a lambing park (using a powerful lamp to identify the predator which can then be cleanly shot) are unselective and cruel.

The fox problem in the Scottish Highlands – if it is a problem and not just a myth in the mind of man – dates from the time of the Clearances which took place mainly in the nineteenth century, when people were removed from the land to make room for vast flocks of sheep. Before that time this predator was a relatively scarce animal, though its numbers were probably slowly building with the demise of the wolf in the early years of the eighteenth century; the wolf would have been a predator competing, in part, for similar prey. With the coming of the sheep, fox numbers must have continued to build, not because the animal had been presented with a bountiful supply of lambs to predate upon, though of course some were taken, but more because sheep casualties resulting from bad weather or disease were not buried or otherwise disposed of, but left lying about. Foxes, eagles, buzzards, wild cats and so on survived on this carrion in the winter months. Increasing numbers of deer, due partly to the extinction of their natural predator the wolf, also meant more carcasses available. Deer stalking began to be popular in Victorian times and the preference for killing stags, leaving the hinds as breeding stock, caused even higher numbers of the animal, and a source of yet more carrion. The practice of leaving grallochs on the hill enabled yet more predators to flourish.

That was the history, and there are a lot of foxes in the Highlands today. In fertile imaginations, and without knowledge of the breeding habits or territorial behaviour of the animal, foxes have multiplied in great numbers and their predation upon lambs, poultry and birds reared for sport has escalated to match. Much of the evidence in the case against the fox is subjective and not based on sound evidence. Nevertheless, in the minds of most sheepfarmers, gamekeepers and sportsmen, the sins of the fox are manifold and any means of despatching it, however inhumanely, are acceptable. Attitudes are much the same in the rest of Britain, and where the ritual of fox hunting on horseback with hounds is practised, attitudes become ferocious and fixed.

The cruelty often involved in controlling so-called pests has in recent years sparked off a protest from the public that grows and will not go away. In 1992 a Bill introduced to the House of Commons by Kevin McNamara, the Member for Kingston upon Hull, North, proposed that it would be an offence to ill-treat cruelly, or intentionally inflict unnecessary suffering on any wild mammal. It was narrowly defeated on Second Reading. Since then pressure from the public and the various bodies concerned with cruelty to animals has continued. In March 1995, as this book goes to print, a similar Bill has been presented by John McFall, the Member for Dumbarton. It has passed its Second Reading and now goes to Committee.

The first three Clauses are the crucial ones:

1. If, save as permitted by this Act, any person cruelly kicks,

beats or tortures any wild mammal, he shall be guilty of an offence.

2. If, save as permitted by this Act, a person wilfully causes any dog to kill, injure, pursue or attack any wild mammal, he shall be guilty of an offence.

3. If, save as permitted by this Act, a person sets any snare for the purpose of killing, injuring or taking any wild mammal, he shall be guilty of an offence.

Various 'let-out' clauses cover special circumstances.

The Bill is highly to be commended in that it would see the end of the hunting of foxes and stags with dogs, and ban the practice of coursing. No longer would terriers be permitted at a fox den, and this would be of considerable significance in Scotland. Snares, too, would be outlawed. These are not only cruel, the animals caught in them suffering appalling deaths, they are also indiscriminate in what they catch. Badger, wild cat and otter are among other victims, and these are protected species. Roe deer are frequently caught and domestic pets, in rural areas, do not escape. The law requires snares that are set to be examined at least once in every twenty-four hours. This is seldom done. It was the contentious Clause 2, however, that occupied Members through the Commons Debate of 3rd March 1995 which lasted for almost five hours, too long to discuss in detail here. Clause 1 was commended because, of course, it was not controversial. Clause 3 received little attention, possibly because it was not relevant to hunting. Clause 2 prompted impassioned speeches from both sides of the House.

Mr McFall put a strong case for his Bill, his main objective to give the same protection to wild mammals as had already been given to domestic mammals under the Protection of Animals Act 1911. He quoted the results of research by reputable scientists and the opinions of honest farmers who admitted that fox predation upon lambs is minimal. He gave accounts of the cruelty which took place in fox and stag hunting, hare coursing, and in the use of snares. He recommended drag hunting as a sport which could well prove as popular as fox hunting, and was already carried on in some parts of the country. He had no objection to humane methods of controlling pests.

While many M.P.s spoke passionately in favour of the Bill, decrying the cruelty as described by Mr McFall, those in the hunting-with-hounds lobby were up in arms. This was the best way to control foxes, they claimed, and also to conserve the species, for the hunts saw to it by various means that there were plenty of foxes to hunt! It was also the best way to ensure a healthy deer population. Country people knew best what was good for the countryside. Evidence of cruel practices the fox hunters maintained, was much exaggerated and did not occur in well-organised hunts. Besides, the rural economy in many parts of the country would be ruined if fox hunting was banned and soon a way of life would be gone forever. This was the thin end of the wedge, and shooting and fishing would go the same way. And so on. The scientific evidence produced by Mr McFall was either ignored or not seriously discussed by any of them.

Nothing seems to change. Once again a Parliamentary debate demonstrates the inescapable fact that those who do not want to know, or are politically motivated not to know, never will know. A lot of research has been carried out on the fox, by Dr David Macdonald in England and Dr Ray Hewson in Scotland (both quoted in the Debate) and others well-qualified, which proves that the fox's predation upon live lambs is infinitesimal. Still-born lambs, or those that are weak and unlikely to survive, are more often taken. There is no need to cull the fox, except in special circumstances. This mammal, in fact, does the farmer a service in predating upon the short-tailed vole and the rabbit, both of which eat a lot of his grazing. We, too, have met honest farmers, here in the Highlands, who admit to little or no damage done by foxes. It must also be significant, and this was mentioned in the Debate, that areas known to be free of foxes, such as the Isle of Mull, suffer the same lamb losses as those that are not.

There are two main reasons for an increase in fox numbers at the present time: one is that unselective methods of control encourage high breeding rates, and the other is that a food supply in winter enables animals, especially last season's cubs, to survive.

We have no objection to the selective and humane control of foxes when necessary and in the right circumstances, such as in a lambing park, nor to the culling of deer by competent and preferably professional stalkers with rifles. In Scotland, the hunting of deer by dogs has been outlawed for nearly forty years.

Acknowledgements

Grateful thanks are due to Tony Colwell, my editor at Jonathan Cape, who has taken endless trouble and given me a great deal of very useful advice whenever I encountered problems in the writing of this book. Sincere thanks are also due to Jean Edwards who, once again, has painstakingly helped with the correction of proofs.

I would also like to offer thanks to all those friends and colleagues who have been prepared to comment on our experience and add to it with their own. To those mentioned in the book I have given pseudonyms, in order that they may be protected from any not so sympathetic neighbours or associates.

Select Bibliography

J. Barrington, *Red Sky at Night*, Michael Joseph, 1984

R. Burrows, *Wild Fox*, David & Charles, 1968

R. F. S. Creed, 'Observations on reproduction in the wild red fox (Vulpes vulpes)', *British Veterinary Journal* 116 (pp.419-26), 1960

J. Crumley, *Badgers on the Highland Edge*, Jonathan Cape, 1994

M. J. W. Douglas, 'Notes on the red fox (Vulpes vulpes) near Braemar, Scotland', *Journal of Zoology* 147 (pp. 228-33), 1956

P. L. Errington & R. M. Berry, 'Tagging studies of red foxes', *Journal of the Mammal Society*, 18 (pp.203-5), 1937

C. Ferris, *Out of the Darkness*, Unwin Hyman, 1988

F. Fraser Darling, *Natural History in the Highlands and Islands*, Collins, 1947

S. Gordon, *The Golden Eagle*, The Melven Press, Perth, 1980

H. G. Hurrel, *The Fox*, Sunday Times Publications, 1962

D. Jenkins, 'The present status of the wild cat (Felis silvestris) in Scotland', *Scottish Naturalist* 70 (pp.126-38), 1962

J. C. Kirk & R. Wagstaffe, 'A contribution to the study of the Scottish Wild Cat', Part I, Size and Weight, *Northwest Naturalist*, 18 (pp.271-5), 143

League Against Cruel Sports, *The Red Fox – Friend or Foe – What the Experts Say*, 1993, excerpts from papers by J. Barrington, R. Burrows, Dr S. Harris, Dr R. Hewson, Dr R. Hewson and A. F. Leitch, Dr R. Hewson and H. H. Kolb, H. G. Lloyd, D. MacCaskill and Dr D. Macdonald.

A. Leutcher, *Tracks and Signs of British Animals*, Cleaver-Hulme Press, 1960

H. G. Lloyd, *The Red Fox*, Batsford, 1980

J. D. Lockie, 'After myxomatosis', *Scottish Agriculturalist* 36 (pp.65-9), 1956

J. D. Lockie, 'Estimation of the food of foxes', *Wildlife Management* 23 (pp.224-7), 1959

Select Bibliography

D. Macdonald, *Running with the Fox*, Unwin Hyman, 1987

L. H. Matthews, *British Mammals*, Collins (New Naturalist), 1952

E. G. Neal, *The Badger*, Collins (New Naturalist), 1948

H. N. Southern, *The Handbook of British Mammals*, Blackwell Scientific Publications, 1941

W. L. Taylor, 'The wild cat (Felis silvestris) in Great Britain', *Journal of Animal Ecology* 8, 6, (pp. 6-9), 1946

H. Tetley, 'On the Scottish Fox', *Proceedings of the Zoological Society, London* 11B (pp. 23-35), 1941

M. Tomkies, *Golden Eagle Years* (revised edition), Jonathan Cape, 1994

M. Tomkies, *Wildcat Haven*, Jonathan Cape, 1987

B. Vesey-Fitzgerald, *Town Fox, Country Fox*, Deutsch, 1965

R. E. Vincent, 'Observations on red fox behaviour', *Ecology* 39 (pp.755-7), 1958

A. Watson, 'The winter food of six Highland foxes', *Scottish Naturalist* 67 (pp. 123-4), 1955

J. E. Wood, 'Relative estimates of fox population levels', *Journal of Wildlife Management* 23 (pp. 53-63), 1959